Orb to Eternity

Alf Jones

DEDICATION

To my late mother Elfrieda

CONTENTS

PREFACE

Having built up a thriving polythene bag manufacturing business, we quickly outgrew the premises we were in, and a decision was reached to move into a larger factory.

After selecting an ideal site from a limited supply in the Yorkshire area, an old disused mill was chosen. The mill was very old, and had before being used by an international engineering group for many years, and previously a cotton mill amongst other things. A beautiful location in a sleepy village, with scope for expansion.

But after moving in we found to our horror that the place was supernaturally alive, what we as a company were about to experience was the last thing we needed.

The events that followed, however, jogged my memory to many other strange occurrences which I had put to the back of my mind, those experiences and others which were to follow have led me into writing this whole strange story.

1 AN OLD FRIEND

For as long as I can remember, I believe that I have always known that someday I would stumble upon the answers to many of life's age-old questions, questions that lurk in the deep recesses of our minds, but are difficult to contemplate, never mind be able to be answered. I believe strongly now, having reached the age of sixty, that it was in my destiny, that I would by nature of events which have followed me through my life, possibly by design – who knows – be in a position to cast light and give answers to the age-old questions to which I refer.

I also believe that by looking at the way I have convinced myself that the visions shown to me in many different forms throughout my life are correct, I am obliged for some unknown reason to put pen to paper, thus sharing with all who want to be enlightened the chance to do so.

There are, as I see it, a myriad of questions that we ask ourselves to which no-one has the answers, such as why do we exist at all on this earth; what is the purpose of life; is there life after death and many, many more, including do our actions on this planet affect our post-death future? Sadly, these only scratch the surface of what we would all like to know.

I can tell you, however, that as I first mentioned, I myself have been experiencing things the whole of my life and also have the benefit of many tales and prophecies passed down to me by my ancestors on my late mother's side of the family, who herself was a medium as well as being the mother of my twin sister and I.

Having briefly described to you my reasons for turning

to the pen after all these years, I must confess that it was only through the reunion with an old friend, whom I had first met several years ago in Ireland, that I found it necessary to relate my story to him, in fact to give solace back to Michael and his family who were experiencing a family illness and were in need of spiritual guidance.

I will now attempt to relate the facts as accurately as I can. You must bear in mind that I am in no way an accomplished writer, but I will attempt to keep your interest whilst writing the true facts.

It was Saturday at last, and after a busy week I was looking forward to doing nothing but spending two days taking it easy, and that meant starting with a good English breakfast. As I headed hungrily towards the kitchen I heard the letter box. More bills, I grumbled, bending down to collect a pile of brown envelopes; yes, I was right: electricity, water rates...ah, but at last a white envelope, and with an Irish stamp.

As I sat down at the breakfast table slowly enjoying my pile of unhealthy ecstasy, I opened the letter and began to read. Crikey, it was from Michael, an old friend of mine who I had met whilst I had been working over in Ireland a few years previously. He was heading over to Yorkshire for a short break with his family; they were booked into a hotel just a few minutes away from where I now lived with my wife and son, and according to the letter they would be here the next day, Sunday. Well, there goes my peaceful rest, we will have to get tided up and invite them over for a meal to repay the hospitality they showed us while we were over in Ireland.

My wife and son, who incidentally was also called Michael and was now ten years old, had gone shopping early that morning allowing me to sleep late and have a steady morning. But I rang my wife on the mobile to pick up some nice cakes and a bottle of wine ready for the arrival of our visitors the next day.

Sunday came and our friends duly arrived as the letter had indicated at the White Lion Hotel. I was there waiting to meet them. It was so nice to see Michael after so long, and I did not waste any time in inviting them to come over to our house.

'You go, Michael,' said Jenny, his wife. 'We are so tired after the journey and the children would rather chill out here and explore the hotel.' Michael agreed and the two of us set off back to my house reminiscing all the way, and making plans for a couple of pints in my local pub.

I must say the temptation of a pint and the need to catch up on three years saw us call straight in the Globe rather than my house, but I did have the decency to ring my good lady to let her know where we were.

We got to the bar quite easily as it was quietening down after the lunchtime rush. The carvery had just closed but sandwiches were still being sold; we ordered two glasses of stout and a selection of cold meat sandwiches with the intention of having an hour and then popping round home for a chat with Tammy and Michael.

It was such a nice afternoon, with plenty to catch up on, in a lovely olde worlde pub with its quaint low oak-beamed bar along with a small log fire burning in the grate, a large plate of sandwiches and free pickles, all washed down with Irish stout, lovely!

I was about to go to the bar for a second glass, when Michael's mobile phone rang, I assumed it would be Jenny enquiring of his whereabouts and possibly his time of return but he seemed to be distressed as he spoke in a low voice whilst turning away to face the window; he got up and continued talking as he went outside, it must have been a good five minutes before he came back in to the room.

'I'm sorry about that, Alf,' he said, 'A bit of bad news from Ireland.'

'Do you want to talk about it,' I enquired, 'or is it personal?'

'Well, yes it is bad news and personal, well not really, it's a family member but Alf, you're just like family anyhow.'

He went on to say that his mother had just been admitted into hospital and could he return to Ireland as soon as possible, as she was very poorly. Apparently she had been ill for some time; she had fallen down on three or four occasions; she suffered from loss of memory and now had the makings of pneumonia.

'It's a shame,' said Michael, 'We really needed this break, the children have had no holiday for ages now, you see, I am always working, but I could also see Jenny was losing weight, so I thought I would take this opportunity while work was slack to grab a couple of weeks away, to do nothing but relax. I never thought for a moment that Mother would get worse; she seems to have been stable for a while now. Do you know, Alf, it's a year since my father passed on and, to be honest, we are all worn out. We had two years of his illness but I think this past year since we buried him has taken more out of us all than the two previous years; it's hard to carry on without such a man, and I can quite understand my mother giving up without him by her side. I must go back to her, Alf, but I just feel for Jenny and the kids. We've just got here and they were so much looking forward to it.'

I mused for a moment, remembering the old man. Even in his late seventies he was on the dance floor every Saturday night; there was always a hearty meal on the table at his home; people from his village respected the old man, who did so much for charity, and he could still drink many of the young men under the table even at his age. He had lived his life as a woodsman, living off the land. They say his tracking skills were so good he could track a banshee.

'Look Michael,' I said, 'I have an idea: leave Jenny and the children to finish their holiday in England. My wife and Michael will keep them amused and take them around; they could go on trips to York and the Dales, in fact lots of places, shopping and whatever they like. After all, you looked after us when we were in Ireland. I could accompany you back over to Ireland to be with your mother, and if she recovers sufficiently you could return with me for whatever is left of the holiday, or if you need to stay in Ireland, I could return and make sure Jenny and the children get back safely to you.'

We agreed that this was a good plan, so after finishing our meal and drinks, we returned to my home to make the arrangements for our trip back to Ireland.

Tammy was quite happy to look out for Jenny and the kids, telling us that she would take them on lots of trips. We weren't to worry about a thing, just concentrate on what we had decided to do.

I took out the map and we decided that we would take the A roads down to Fishguard, using the motorways only when necessary. At least that way Michael would see some nice countryside and the stops would be more interesting; there's nothing worse to me than motorway services. So it was down to the garage, to check the oil and water, purchase a full tank of petrol and remember to phone Ireland to let them know of our arrangements. I took Michael back to his hotel as it was now early Sunday evening and made arrangements to pick him up at first light Monday morning.

The next day I set off early to collect Michael from his hotel; as I arrived the family were just going in to breakfast and although I had eaten at home I ate a small bacon and egg meal with them; after all it may be a while before we eat again, I thought. Half an hour later and we were off, heading down towards Manchester where we intended to turn left and take the A49 all the way down to Shropshire, Hereford, Ross on Wye, then pick up the A40 through Wales to the ferry port of Fishguard. A long journey but beautiful scenery all the way and hopefully not too much traffic this way.

I suppose I expected Michael to be his usual chirpy self, but he was far from it; he seemed gloomy, but in view of his worrying about his mother I suppose I could understand that. However I continued to coax him into conversation and eventually despite being extremely subdued he finally apologised for being quiet and told me that he had been thinking of much more than just his mother's situation.

'Look Alf, it's not just that my mother has been taken ill, that I am so upset, but since Dad died last year Mother has been inconsolable and to be honest it's left me thinking about things a lot. Things have been running through my head which you don't normally dwell on, and I can't help it.' 'Thinking what, Michael?' I enquired tentatively as we approached yet another set of road works with its usual two-mile queue. There was a long pause, then he turned towards me, 'I have really tried to be there for my mother since Dad died, but you know how it is, a man has to work, Jenny works part time at the children's school; she does the dinners as well as Playground Monitor. The money at the moment is not so good in Ireland, and the garage does not make as much as it used to, so I have to work longer hours. Then the family are to see to, the house repairs and so on, I just don't have a lot of spare time. And now I feel that I somehow should have found more time to spend with Mother especially with Dad dying so suddenly.

'The thing is,' he paused again, 'Alf, it's only when something like this happens that you look at yourself. I was so busy looking out for the wife and children that I left Mother alone too much. My wife though, has been a real rock, she knew we were having it tough since the 'Celtic tiger' came off the rails and really supported me. I feel I could have done more for Mother just as Jenny has done for me.'

Michael's wife Jenny was a lovely, absolutely typical Southern Irish Colleen, brought up in the old Irish traditions, part of a family of twelve children, growing most of their own food on a small farm no more than one acre and a half. She was always full of vitality, clean and god-fearing. She would be up in the morning as the cock crowed to see to breakfast and then sort out the children to ready them for school. Next came a full day's work which included her duties at the school along with housework, shopping, seeing to the fourteen hens they kept and any small repair jobs around the house. I suppose that was also one of the reasons Michael had insisted she completed her well deserved holiday along with the children, as he well knew she needed the change as well as the rest.

Finally we were out of the roadworks and on our way again. As we travelled along the roads out of Yorkshire towards Manchester on the first leg of our journey, I kept up a good commentary about the moorland and countryside that we passed through, illustrating to Michael how severe the winters were up on these lonely moors and recalling tales I had heard of some of the strange hermit types that used to live up here on the sparsely scattered crofts. I suppose I had noticed that Michael had again become a bit subdued and I felt I had to make conversation.

'Oh sorry,' Michael whispered, 'I was drifting a bit then, what were you saying?'

'Oh it's OK, Michael, it might do you well to have a doze,' I replied.

'No I can't. My mind, you see, it just won't rest. I just can't get Mother out of my thoughts, she's been so upset since Dad died. It's been a year now and it's not got any easier for her, she talks of him constantly, and she looks so terribly sad. It's also starting to make me think that her illness is a direct link to my father's passing, that she is in fact giving up; what do you think, Alf?'

Well, I felt a bit awkward and tried to console Michael, but he had managed to get himself so depressed that I found it difficult. I did, however, point out to him that I had been a close family friend for a good number of years now, and that I had come to know his father as a truly good, kind and generous man; he had looked after his family and was totally god-fearing. In fact if anyone on this earth deserved eternal life it was him. I went on to say that I believed fully that he had in fact begun his journey to the next life with not a regret, and my expectation that his still-living wife would join him in due course.

'In fact, Michael,' I went on, 'I have a feeling that your mother is probably of the same mind and this may have some bearing on her illness, in some ways wanting to rejoin him.'

Michael took a sideways look towards me. 'Alf, that's very profound, you speak as if you are sure there is something to come after death. You speak with such conviction; can it be that Dad is still around, just in another place; is that what you are saying?'

Now then, Michael's words surprised me somewhat. I was very aware through my experiences of life that this mortal life was only a small part of our existence, but somehow I naively believed that others held the same beliefs probably based on similar experiences to those which I had been lucky enough to have witnessed.

It started to dawn on me, however, that this was probably not the case and that the enormous amount of privileged knowledge that I had collected through my life regarding our past, present and future existence was maybe only really known and understood by a few, of which I was lucky enough to be one.

Now then I had to think quickly; obviously what I am talking about and what I believed most people to have some knowledge of was not common to us all, so did I now divulge to Michael this revelation, for want of a more suitable word? Yes, the answer had to be yes: this explanation that I was in a position to put forward to him, I hoped would go a long way to settling his mind and to showing him the way through life.

'Michael, I think that it would be good for us both if I now explain to you things which I believe will benefit you, in so far as our spiritual and earthly existence. What I have to say to you is, I have an explanation of why we are here on Earth, also of its effects and of what occurs after death. You will find what I am about to explain to you in some cases hard to understand but if you allow me to tell you my story from start to finish I think you will be a very informed, spiritually content person, capable of handling situations that you now find yourself in with regard to your mother.'

Michael nodded, so I continued. 'Throughout my life, Michael, I have been very privileged to have gained a tremendous knowledge of what some may term spiritual or in some cases supernatural; I actually consider it 'a truth'.

'I have had my eyes opened by means of encounters, dreams, premonitions and varying forms of messages which have come to me in all sorts of ways. These dreams, encounters, premonitions and sometimes passed-down information, started with me from a very early age and have been there in some shape or form all through my life, sometimes more constant than others but pointing me towards a truth or understanding of which I feel it has been my destiny to know, and that now I believe I have to pass on to others. The reason, I don't know: perhaps to warn those who are to follow of what is to come or merely, as in this case, to give solace to someone. Well whatever the reason, Michael, listen to my story and I hope you will then understand as I do where we come from, what we are and where we are going, indeed the old question of what is life all about.'

I must point out that trying to relate my story to Michael and drive through this beautiful moorland scenery was quite a task as I had obviously to keep concentrating on the road. After all, we did not want an accident. So it came as a bit of a relief when we came to a small roadside cafe. I pulled in to the gravel-covered car park, we got out of the car and stretched our legs.

'Right,' said Michael, 'a nice pot of tea, a sandwich and that small table just outside the cafe entrance, that's what appeals to me at the moment.' I agreed as we strode into the quaint but virtually empty countryside tea room.

Within a matter of a few minutes we were sat outside in the afternoon sunshine enjoying our snack. It was a little gem of a place, nestling amongst a fountain of roses with the backdrop of the moorland hills giving shelter, and not many patrons, just ourselves and one other couple. The cakes were just as good, covered in pink icing, just the way I like them.

As Michael tucked into his second cake I went on with my story. After all, there was a lot to tell and I was hoping to get through the account before our arrival at Fishguard.

'Michael, it may seem strange to you, that I have taken it upon myself to explain such strange things to you in this way, but one of the reasons is that I know that you are still devastated by your father's passing and now find yourself worrying about your mother. That is why I am telling you my innermost private secrets and thoughts even though I find it somewhat embarrassing. In fact some people hearing my tale would think I was deranged but you have known me a long time now, and I hope you know that I would never lie or exaggerate the truth. No, my story is absolutely the truth.

'I need you to know, Michael, that your father will be enormously happy now. He has moved through to the next adventure that is in all our destinies. I say in all our destinies but I must point out that it is at this point, 'our passing' that many different roads can be taken and it is based on our time on Earth as to which of these roads we go down. Now your father was, as I mentioned earlier, a good, kind god-fearing family man, he would help anyone in need if he could, and never hurt anyone, a truly good human being who I feel sure will now be at peace.'

Michael listened to me attentively and without interruption, I could see that he was extremely interested in what I had to say. This encouraged me to tell him everything, even though some parts made me feel uneasy and slightly embarrassed.

Time was not on our side, though. We had already spent a good half hour in the tea room, and in front of us was still the bulk of the journey.

'Come on Michael,' I said, reluctantly heaving myself off the chair, 'We're still on the wrong side of Manchester, let's try to get onto the A49 and get down as far as possible to Hereford before we make another stop.'

Michael agreed, so after settling our bill and a quick visit to the wash room, we were once more back on the road.

I now continued with the next part of my story, and it is interesting now to point out that I felt I must begin the tale at a point in my life when quite a major set of circumstances caused me to reflect back over my entire life, to come to the conclusion I have now reached.

I can honestly say, Michael, that it was a particular strange chain of events which happened to me several years ago when I was in my later forties that caused me to reflect over the whole of my life and now leads me to believe that I have figured out what I have come to call 'the Truth'.

'The Truth', I must press upon you again as I see it, also involves where we come from, our purpose of being given life and where we are to go following our death. I genuinely believe I have had my eyes opened to this truth, and I will now start to relate to you the story.

I had in my teenage years been trained by means of an apprenticeship to become an electrician. I worked until my early twenties with the local electricity supply industry, but took it upon myself to study power electronics, which in those days was a fast-moving science with only a small amount of young men taking up that type of training. It did, however, help me to secure a job in an equally forward-thinking industry of the manufacture of polythene. This technology was in its infancy, so between the science of polythene along with my electrical, mechanical and electronic background I soon found myself working for a multinational company with a very good technical job. Over the years I learnt the business of polythene bag making, also the machinery required to do the job, I also understood well the molecular science of the plasmoulds and how to construct the different polymers to create good products.

Eventually it was inevitable that I ended up with my own factory, which I ran along with a lifelong family friend who was a brilliant engineer and salesman.

We started business in a small factory area, no more than 7,000 square feet but quickly outgrew the premises, so it was decided to move our huge machines to new premises which formed part of an old large industrial complex.

The new manufacturing sheds we had taken covered an area of about 50,000 square feet, so having plenty of room for expansion we quickly doubled the amount of machines that had moved with us. Along with the doubling of capacity came more staff, who, alongside the trained staff we had brought with us, we were able to find locally and train up ourselves.

The manufacture of polythene bags involves a continual process operation due to the time it takes for the larger metal dies, sometimes weighing up to a tonne, to heat up to a constant temperature and for the plastic to melt evenly through the dies. It can take up to a day before the extruder settles down to give constant gauge and melt flow. The last thing you want is to be turning the machines off for no reason; it would be not only a loss of production time but also a loss of material, attempting to restabilise the machines. Therefore the staff have to work shifts, covering days and nights, seven days a week. In fact the only time we shut the machines down was at Christmas and then the engineers would carry out essential maintenance work, which would mean the factory never closed.

We also ran a small side business, supplying chemicals and paper products to the cleaning industry. The intention of this was to promote our own bag sales at a slightly higher margin but also to support the enormous cash flow required to run our manufacturing business. The chemical supply part of the company ran from the same premises and in doing so its overheard cost recovery was low. In fact, it had no wage bill as my partner's wife did the paperwork and most of the order taking.

The two-pronged attack of our manufacturing and supply business helped us into the cash and carry supply, along with small supermarkets down to nursing homes, caravan parks and even polythene sheeting for the building industry. In fact we got so busy that I found myself in a position that I had to work night shift myself to help get out the massive volumes of orders for bags which were coming in.

I would through the late part of that first summer at the new factory begin work at 7pm and work right through the night till 9am, six nights every week. They were terribly long nights but it was amazing what production I could turn out; I mean I never stopped the machine I was running and it was noticed that the other bag machine operators' outputs also increased. I think they may have been trying to compete with me.

Anyhow Michael, I digress.

2 THE FACTORY

It was during the early part of the evening of my first night shift in our new surroundings within the industrial complex that very odd things started to happen. Strange things, little by little began to give me cause for concern, until these events built up into a flow of weird happenings.

I do, however, remember that first evening as if it were yesterday. It was a Tuesday; I had prepared well for my first night shift, bringing with me lots of savoury and sweet snacks, my thinking being that I could stay at my machine all night to gain the maximum output by keeping it producing as much as possible by eating at the machine rather than shutting down to go eat in the canteen.

It was on one of the tea breaks when the rest of the operators had gone to the canteen, that I had my first inkling that there was something amiss. The machine I was running was a Falcon roll bag machine, the idea being that an eighty kilogram parent reel of polythene tube was loaded onto the unwind stand at the back of the Falcon; the tube was then threaded through a series of rollers along the length of the machine which included a sealing and perforation unit, firstly arriving at the operator, or front end of the machine, where after being folded and counted the bags would index through in neat rolls of twenty. It was my job then to put a label round the completed roll and drop it into a box. The Falcon machine itself was no more than one metre wide but was a good five metres in length.

It was usual practice to use the sides of the machine as shelves, to rest Sellotape, small tools such as knives or Allen keys or even paperwork, as they were handy for when changing the parent reel and keeping note of the production figures. But it was to my astonishment when, out of the corner of my eye, I saw a Stanley knife blade jump up off the side of the machine and land a good metre away, on the concrete floor.

I could not believe it. I pondered on this for some time, eventually putting the cause as being static electricity building up in the machine. Surely it could not possibly throw the blade such a distance, but what else could cause such a thing?

I slowly convinced myself that the polythene films moving through the machine at high speed over so many rollers might be able to build up sufficient charge to catapult a thin, light piece of metal such as a blade, but that theory soon went out of the window when a long reach 6 millimetre Allen key decided to play the same trick. I was so bemused by this latest occurrence that I stopped the machine and bent over to pick up both the blade and the Allen key. As I bent over I heard what sounded like the voices of children, coming from the wall behind the row of converting bag machines. They seemed to be in the room with me and it seemed as though there were many of them there. I could also hear the sound of carts rolling along the factory floor; you would imagine the carts to have wooden wheels. It went quiet, as quickly as I moved towards the wall I heard no more, but there was a strange smell of wool in the air. I turned and saw the evening staff returning from the canteen and decided not to mention to anyone what I had just witnessed for fear of upsetting some of them needlessly.

At this point of my story, Michael, I think it would be a good idea to give you a mental layout of the factory. Imagine, if you can, a square approximately 200 feet by 200 feet with a metal dividing wall running down its length. This effectively creates two sheds; the left one looking down the sheds from the office and canteen area was used for warehousing and the right-hand shed, again looking down the length of the sheds with your back to the offices, canteen and WC was the production area, of which the farthest 100 feet had the heavy twenty foot high polythene extruders in a line of eleven, and the 100 feet nearest to the canteen and main road housed the twelve light bag machines along with air compressors, workshop and the main entrance.

The metal fabricated wall which ran right down the middle of the sheds' length was manufactured from light gauge tin held in position by two inch angle iron, and the left-hand shed which was used as a warehouse for raw materials and finished goods was about six foot lower in floor level, as the sheds all down that side of the tractor plant were terraced so any movement of materials between the sheds had to be by means of lifting, normally using forklift trucks.

As I explained in the layout, the right-hand shed housed the production machines, and the 'bottom', farthest away from the office 100 feet housed the extruders. An extruder is the first stage of the making of polythene bags and is constructed of a loading hopper into which 'polymer' or beads of polythene are put after being blended for colour and material type. The hopper drops the beads into an Archimedes screw which is heated to around 200 degrees Centigrade. As the polymer travels through the rotating screw it melts and is pushed under pressure through a ninety degree bend and up through a filter into a round die. As the melted film emerges from the die it is blown into a tube by means of compressed air coming through the centre, dragged about twenty feet into the air before being trapped between two closed rollers. By this time the polythene has cooled and can be brought down to a winder at floor level and rolled into eighty kilo rolls ready to be 'doffed' to go to the bag machines. An average weight of one of these extruders would be a total of five tonnes.

As I noted earlier, the extruders take a long time to warm up to the correct temperature and even longer to settle down, allowing the finished polythene tube to be consistent when produced. It is therefore imperative to keep the machines running; it is also essential to have good operation and decent shift patterns so we used a continental pattern of twelve hour nights and days, four on then four off. Shifts would start at 8am till 8pm then 8pm till 8am. The big machines, however, were staffed days, evenings and nights Monday to Friday only, as they outran the extruders.

That, Michael, gives you an idea how the factory worked, apart from one important fact, that being the office. It was built on top of the canteen and WCs and having windows both on the road side looking out onto the front yard, and on the factory side, anyone looking down the factory had a bird's eye view of the production activity right down to the back fire door at the end of the extrusion department.

Anyway, to get back to the story of my first night shift, the time had moved on to 10pm; the evening shift girls were clocking out and heading home, meanwhile three night-shift machine operators were clocking in ready for their ten hour shifts. It was usual to employ men for this night shift and girls for the evening shift of 5pm till 10pm, but for no other reason than it was the way the staff had sorted themselves out.

The night shift extrusion operator this particular night was Steven; he was a man with a great knowledge of polythene production. Having been in the business some ten years and specialising only on the raw material production side, he nevertheless was capable of helping out on the bag machine production if required to do so. Steven would work over and above the shift time just to help the company; he was a real hard worker, with the company always taking first priority. Steven was also a fairly strait-laced kind of guy but also loved a joke provided it hurt no-one. So it was Steven I first confided in. I watched for him to amble up the shed to the canteen area, probably with the intention of making his first pot of tea since coming in to work. I quickly turned off the Falcon machine that I was running and went up the shed to talk to him.

Sure enough, Steven was standing by the wooden staircase which accessed the overhead office, stirring his pint pot of weak tea.

'Hi Steven, first time tonight I have had the chance to talk to you,' I shouted as I walked towards him. You had to raise your voice, as the noise of the machinery was rumbling away, making sign language between the operators quite common, when working several metres apart.

I took the opportunity to share a few minutes with Steven in the canteen where it was much quieter, although I just helped myself to a paper cup of coffee from the free issue drinks machine rather than waste time brewing fresh tea. It was during these few minutes that I confided in him of the strange happenings of the previous couple of hours, and obviously with Steven working night shift regularly I asked, had he noticed anything out of the ordinary, not expecting an affirmative answer.

You can imagine my surprise when he said without hesitation, 'Oh yes, lots of weird things, but I try to put them out of my mind. You see, I work at night alone quite often and it doesn't do to dwell on these things.'

Steven went on to say that he first thought he was imagining what was going on around him, but over the weeks came to expect the odd 'shock', as he called it. He was also, I think, a bit relieved that someone else had finally had some similar experiences; it proved to him that he wasn't 'losing it'.

Steven went on to recount one or two incidents but due to the fact that his extruder needed attention such as raw materials to be topped up in the hoppers and finish product reels of film to be taken off the machines he could not go into great detail. Besides, I was short of time as my production figures would suffer. Needless to say, he did recall the first couple of incidents.

It was one Sunday night several weeks previously when, whilst sitting on a stool by the side of Number Three extruder to change the filter, he had a feeling that the temperature had plummeted. In fact he felt cold, and saying that he was working amongst a row of extruders which all ran in excess of 200 degrees Centigrade and each with a usage of at least fifty kilowatts, that was quite surprising. But nevertheless Steven pushed on with the filter change, not wanting to keep the extruder stopped too long.

The changing of the filter on this particular type of extruder meant taking out six twelve millimetre four inch long bolts using a large Allen key, then removing the filter block from the side of the filter unit. The block was then cleaned with a brass brush and replaced after installing a fresh gauze filter. Finally refitting the six bolts.

It was when Steven came to replace the six bolts that on looking into the wooden tray containing his filter change kit that he found that all six bolts had gone. He distinctly remembered cleaning each bolt as it was withdrawn from the hot filter block and applying graphite grease ready for its being refitted, then laying them in the wooden box so that they would not roll away, or worse roll under the extruder barrel.

Steven looked all around the machine but no, they had gone, and being Sunday night, there was no-one in the building with him, in other words not another living soul to move them without his knowledge. Steven was a tad shaken but instinct sent him off to the workshop for a fresh set of bolts. As he walked past the winder at the front of the extruder he had been working on he heard a noise behind him and on turning to face Number Two extruder he witnessed a winder reel bar rise from the ground and throw itself into the middle of the alleyway, at least three metres in distance and probably two metres into the air. It came down with a crash, not surprisingly because the weight of the reel bar along with its winding cones would be in the region of twenty five kilograms. This now began to unsettle Steven, but in spite of this latest shock he managed to soldier on through the night shift without further incidents.

The next night, however, Steven was in better spirits due to there being a full shift on nights, so the feeling of looking over your shoulder as the night before, wondering what was going to befall you next seemed not to be an issue, until on changing the filter again on extruder Number Three, he reached the point of replacing the bolts. Tonight, though, Steven had taken particular notice of the greased bolts going into the box. Imagine his surprise when, turning to pick up the first bolt having placed the filter block into position, there were twelve bolts in the box and on picking them up he found six were still hot with the grease running through the threads, but six were stone cold with the grease on the threads solid.

Apart from these incidents Steven went on to say there had been small but insignificant occurrences, but only things which could be put down to your imagination having witnessed the aforesaid events, and in saying that, he did not expand any further on these matters.

Now then, Michael, as you can understand having myself witnessed some odd goings on and hearing what Steven had to say, I thought it prudent to keep notes, thinking that if there were any further revelations I would not only have a record, but could compare them with earlier dates and times of similar happenings should they occur.

How right I was to keep a record because it seemed to me that now we were aware that something was going on, whatever was causing the things to happen now went into overdrive.

Over the course of the next four days I was plagued by strange noises, sudden drops in temperature, voices of children, the sounds of carts and unfamiliar machinery, strange smells and all manner of unseen provocations. But worse was to come and it came in the form of an apparition. I had managed to just about complete my first week on night shift; it was now Friday night and approaching meal time, that is midnight. I turned off my machine and called out to Andrew who was on his first night of extrusion shift that I would put the kettle on; he signalled OK from the bottom of the shed, holding up five fingers to signify 'give me five minutes'.

I wandered up to the canteen, passing the row of bag machines which were stood idle due to there not being a conversion shift on Friday, Saturday or Sunday nights. In other words, there was just myself and Andrew in the building. As I approached the door of the canteen something caught my eye. I glanced to my left and there, stood at the foot of the wooden staircase which led up to the first floor office door, was an orange glowing shape in the shape of a hooded figure. I stared in disbelief as it slowly faded away. There were no features to the figure, just a hooded long-gowned orange shape of a person stood between the bottom of the staircase and the Gents toilet door; no noise, no smell, nothing. I shuddered and remembered that I was going to call into the WC before settling down to my sandwiches. I decided to give the WC a miss and on top of that I had lost my appetite. I made do with a strong pot of coffee with plenty of sugar instead.

Andrew was amazed that I had no appetite and to be honest I felt it prudent not to let him know what I had just witnessed nor indeed what had been going on all week. After all, he would be working alone the next two nights and I did not want to spook him.

We had our half hour in the canteen but Andrew had to run down the shed quickly when Number Six extruder developed a problem, in so far as the polythene tube lost size; this can be caused when a small bit of carbon gets through the filter and punctures the hot polythene as it leaves the die on its cooling run up to the nip rollers high in the air.

I set off to follow him down the shed but remembered that I should call at the WC and on top of that I had drunk not one, but two cups of coffee, I gingerly tiptoed into the Gents but saw nothing, no orange shapes. I relaxed but only for a moment, as a deep, low, warm voice spoke right into my left ear.

'OOOH Alf.' It was as if someone was standing next to me and had leaned over and quietly spoken right into my ear. I panicked: there was no sign of anyone or anything apart from the voice. I was soon running down the shed to the extruder operator.

'Crikey,' Andrew blurted, 'You made me jump, Alf, what's wrong?' I made the excuse that I thought he needed help to rectify the extruder fault, I actually felt a bit silly, surprisingly, after all was it possible I had imagined it? I don't think!

The rest of that Friday night went without a hitch, but I can tell you I was happy to exit the factory on Saturday morning. And, do you know, the sun was out and the light of day made the previous night's events feel just like a dream.

My weekend seemed to fly past, what with my trying to catch up on sleep after five very long night shifts, coupled with the weekly shopping and making a good a promise to my wife of a shopping trip for curtains for the new house we had recently moved into, time just disappeared.

Nevertheless, the thought of my second week of night shift was filled with anticipation, intrigue and in some way a little dread as to what I may now encounter.

In some ways the anticipation of further weird events happening seemed to match the importance of trying to catch up on the backlog of production, which was after all the primary reason for me working the night shift in the first place.

Monday night was soon upon me. I arrived at the factory slightly early so as to discuss both the forthcoming night's output requirement along with a rough overview of the week's schedule. This discussion was with my business partner whose job was generally to look after sales and marketing. At this time, may I add, I had decided not to mention the strange events of the previous week for fear of attracting unwanted ridicule. I had, however, confided in Andrew with what I witnessed and, being Monday night, it was Andrew's last shift looking after the extruders, so once the evening shift girls had begun production on their allotted machines, I ventured down the shed to have a word with him, mainly to ask whether or not there had been any more events over the weekend.

Andrew told me that he had indeed witnessed a couple of small unexplained episodes but apart from those, nothing else.

The episodes he was referring to were catching sight of a dark shape moving amongst the extruders whilst at the same time a sudden drop in temperature, and the crying of children's voices, exactly as I had explained to him the previous Friday.

He also went on to tell me that the happenings were becoming common knowledge and that most of the staff had encountered something, but had preferred to keep quiet, each fearing ridicule.

However, some were now talking quite openly, may I say, and it wasn't long before many stories were coming to my attention. Not only were the stories becoming common knowledge between the workforce, but news travels fast and it wasn't long before the other businesses on our site were aware of what was being experienced in our factory.

That second week became quite an active one for our supernatural tenants. During the week I saw a multitude of strange things. For instance, whilst walking amongst the line of extruders I saw small grey clouds dancing among the machines, a couple of metres from the ground. They would float around then move quite quickly left, right or sometimes vertically, disappearing as quickly as they came, sometimes to be replaced by small round floating balls of light also dancing amongst the machines, I noticed that when this phenomenon happened it usually coincided with a sharp drop in temperature.

It was while I was experiencing something of the sort on the Tuesday evening that I mentioned it to Thomas, who was starting his first night of four twelve-hour shifts. To my astonishment he went on to tell me that he had experienced many such things whilst working for us; he also told me that he had seen a figure of a man walking in the lower shed, which we used as a warehouse, one weekend. Thomas thought it was strange as he was the only person in the place and besides that the doors were locked. He decided to confront the figure and called out; the figure took no notice but walked towards the higher level shed where the extruders were running.

'Well,' said Thomas, 'you can imagine my horror when the figure walked straight into the higher level, all I could see was his shoulders and head, gliding across the floor, under the extruders and then finally disappearing into the wall on the next higher level,' which was occupied by a toy manufacturing company. It was obviously a ghost, he said, and the possible reason it walked into the higher level was that at sometime in the past the floor must have been all one level, that would mean he had seen something from the distant past. I asked Thomas if he could describe the man but the only thing he could recall was that the figure looked gaunt, rather dirty, wearing a flat cloth cap and dark blue overalls, which appeared to be made from very thick material.

I went back to my machine, and began to try to make sense of it all as I began to plough into the long night's production requirement, but try as I might to stick to the running of my machine I was constantly given a running commentary from various members of staff right through the night on odd things they were hearing and seeing. I was beginning to think that I had somehow initiated a form of hysteria, when at around 4am there was an almighty banging noise. It sounded as if someone was beating the long twelve-foot-high tin dividing wall which separated the lower warehouse shed from the upper production shed where I was busy running my machine. It went on for three or four minutes; myself and the staff stared in amazement. The noise was deafening but strangely enough there was no sign of anyone on either side of the divider, neither was there any sign of movement of the tin which you would expect given the ferocity of the noise.

The terrible deafening row stopped as suddenly as it had started; there was silence apart from the gentle whirring noise of the polythene extruders. All the bag machines had been stopped by the operators who now stood motionless, staring in disbelief at the tin wall.

I decided it would be a good time for a break and instructed everyone to make their way up to the canteen and that I would stand them all a hot drink, now that the free vend machine was free no more.

Thomas was the last to arrive, 'I have some more bad news for you,' he whispered.

Well whatever it was, I thought, it can't be much worse that what we have all just witnessed, but in a way it was. You see, a motor gearbox which drives the top rollers on Number Five extruder had seized up and was in need of a new set of bearings. I knew that I would not have the time to repair the equipment and keep the urgently required production running. So I decided to call in a friend of mine who although he had a full time job would be able to accomplish the task one evening after finishing his shift.

On leaving the factory that Wednesday morning I made

a point of phoning Philip even before I arrived home. I caught him just as he was about to leave for work and he readily agreed to repair the gear box that same evening although he thought it could be close to midnight before he could get there.

That was good enough for me; we could manage without the machine's production for the odd day but Thursday morning it would really need to be running to as to keep us somewhere near our production schedule.

I slept heavily that day, it was proving to be a very busy week, work or other things were constantly on my mind, so it felt like an escape just to fall asleep for a while. All good things come to an end, however, and it was back to the grindstone, but at least I didn't have to repair the extruder. I counted my blessings that Philip would be soon doing that hot, dirty job.

Strangely enough that night went quietly with no incidents at all. The morning came and I could not remember a night such as we had just enjoyed, where everything had run as clockwork, and without any poltergeist activity. I went up to the canteen with the rest of the tired night shift. Thomas made me a drink, pointing out that he was now off shift for four whole days but then mentioned that Number Five extruder was still not repaired.

Crikey, I had forgotten completely about the gearbox. Where was Philip, why hadn't he come in to repair it? I jumped straight onto the telephone, quickly dialling, to catch him before he left his home to get to his day job.

Philip answered the phone and assured me that he had indeed come as promised to repair the said motor gearbox unit.

He went on to relate a tale to me which cancelled out my earlier exuberance about having an incident-free night. Philip went on to explain to me that he had arrived at around eleven-thirty, and upon parking his car next to the loading bay door he was let in by two of the night shift operators who were slipping out for a crafty cigarette.

He carried his tool box and the new set of bearings down to the extruder to be repaired and made his way up the iron steps to the top platform where the faulty gearbox unit sat, twenty feet up in the air.

There wasn't much room to work so Philip had to position himself with the gearbox unit in front of him, and the tool box and spare bearings behind at the top of the iron staircase.

After cleaning the unit of months of grease and lint with some old rags and white spirit, the fixing bolts had to be loosened off, but as he turned round to take an adjustable spanner from his toolbox, it was handed to him.

'Thank you,' said Philip turning back to the gearbox, and then froze. He spun round to see nothing, no one was there. He looked down the iron staircase, again nothing, and even if he had seen someone they could not have run down in a matter of seconds. He was rooted to the spot.

Eventually Philip stood up, closed his toolbox and left, the job not having been done.

I listened to his story and to be honest, I knew he was telling me the truth. He also informed me that he would not be returning to do the job either. I did however agree with him that he had more than likely encountered our unwelcome tenant. Upon asking him to describe the spectre Philip went on to tell me that the man who passed him the adjustable spanner was gaunt, unshaven, wearing a greasy cloth cap and thick blue heavy overalls. Oh yes, and he noticed the man was wearing leather boots with leather laces. In fact a pretty near description of the figure in the warehouse who had been seen walking into the higher level production shed.

Over the following week or two I made the necessary repairs to the extruder that Philip had left unrepaired, and by working long night shifts which sometimes included weekends I managed to get on top of the backlog of orders. It was therefore with great relief that I reverted back to a normal day shift.

I was glad to be back on the day shift for many reasons, but the one bonus as I saw it was that there would be fewer spooky occurrences. How wrong I was.

My first Monday back on the day shift saw me busily sorting out production schedules, making repairs to machines and servicing the compressor. I also had need of the local electric motor repair company as our spare extruder motor was in need of repair; it only took a few minutes after telephoning the repair company before Tony arrived to pick up the said motor.

I greeted him at the door and invited him for a coffee because as well as being the manager in charge of motor repairs at his company Tony had been a friend of mine for years; in fact I had been a friend of his father's years before I knew Tony.

We ambled into the canteen and I began to make two large mugs of sweet tea. It did not take long, though, before Tony started to take the mickey out of me about our resident ghost. News travels fast, especially news like ours, and it was soon apparent that he had got hold of most of the facts not only from our own traumatised employees but from other workers who were employed in different businesses around the site.

There was only one table in the small canteen; it was six feet long and about two feet wide with six chairs round it, two on each long side, one at the top and one at the bottom.

I placed Tony's pot of tea at the top side of the table and he duly sat down to wait for it to cool down, but meanwhile I stood at the other end of the table with my back to the canteen door, holding my tea as I liked to sip the tea while it was hot.

Tony chortled and laughed as he ridiculed some of the

stories which he had been told and I tried my best to explain to him that it was all true, even though some of the things he had heard sounded farfetched.

'I don't believe one word of it,' he laughed, 'and I will never believe it until I see it myself,' he went on.

Then, as if on cue, his pint pot of tea started to move, and as if it were being pushed by an invisible hand the tea moved slowly the length of the whole six feet of table and stopped right at the other end, where I was sitting.

Tony stood up, his face ashen and looking shocked. He stammered, 'That's it, I'm off.' He left post haste and never again after that incident did he ever enter our premises.

I must also at this point explain that the table was perfectly flat and dry, there was no earthly reason that the pot of tea should react that way save to answer Tony in some spooky sort of way.

As the evening approached that day, I was busy preparing twenty pallets of finished goods ready for loading. The wagon was due at six o' clock and it was always a good idea to get plenty of pallet wrap around the five-feet-high pallets of bags so as to make it safer when loading with the fork truck on the road outside, bearing in mind that the road had quite a steep incline.

Dennis the labourer was supposed to be helping me to prepare the pallets for loading, but after hearing the latest odd story about Tony and the pot of tea had decided it would be more fun to have a laugh at my experience. After all, he had experienced nothing at all, not so much as a glimpse, so why should he believe the rest of us?

Dennis was in reality a good strong lad of twenty years old. He had been with us from the first day of business, helping to install the machines and over the course of time learning how to both run and repair the bag machines. He was most useful when it came to using the forklift truck; he seemed a natural so it became his responsibility to both unload raw materials when they arrived and load finished goods onto outward-going wagons, making sure the paperwork was always in order.

Yes he was, although classed as a labourer, multitalented and I knew he would make a good all-round operator one day, but having said all that, he could easily push the wrong buttons with me, consistently ridiculing myself and others of the staff with jibes about spookies.

It was around five-thirty, the wagon for London would be with us soon and there were still ten pallets left to wrap. I brought yet another box of pallet wrap up out of the warehouse and walked up the shed past the extruders towards the loading bay door, which was to the right of the canteen.

As I headed up the long shed I spotted Dennis. He was looking down towards me, dancing about with his arms floating about trying to impersonate a ghostly character. 'Wooo wooo, is that yoooo?' he chanted in between huge silly laughs.

'Dennis,' I snapped, 'will you get those pallets wrapped; the wagon will be here anytime now.'

Dennis laughed again but obeyed. I left him to the task, choosing to have a word with the extruder operator rather than assist in the wrapping.

Only a couple of minutes had passed when Dennis with a very frightened expression on his face came running down the shed towards me.

'I believe you, I believe you, Alf, I believe you now,' he blurted out. 'I've seen it, just as you said, there is something here.'

I calmed him down, and asked him to tell me exactly what had occurred in the relatively short time between his leaving me to walk up to the finished goods area. After all, it could have been no more than five minutes.

Dennis explained that after having had his fun in taking the mickey out of me to the point of me getting annoyed, that he had wandered back to the finished goods area with the intention of completing the wrapping of the remaining pallets of finished goods.

Upon his arrival at the first pallet, something caught his eye. It looked like a figure amongst the already wrapped pallets which were awaiting the wagon's arrival ready for loading. The strange thing about the figure was that the face, which appeared to be hooded, had no facial features and the whole figure seemed to be made up of dozens of tiny sparkly lights.

Then the figure started to move towards him, darting sideways then forward through the pallets. Dennis panicked and ran down the shed but as he arrived to tell me what was happening, the spectre disappeared.

Now then, I had actually seen the same spectre that Dennis had now obviously encountered, but I had never spoken of this particular sparkly light apparition to a soul, so it confirmed to me that Dennis had really in truth had seen an apparition, just as I myself had seen it on two or three occasions and always at the top of the shed, near to where I had witnessed the first sighting of an orange figure floating about near the bottom of the wooden office staircase some weeks previously.

Following this event, we seemed to have regular encounters most evenings and nights. Happenings usually began after 6pm but from time to time the odd daytime encounter could be witnessed.

I did notice, however, that there seemed to be an increase in the number of grey clouds or mists floating amongst the extrusion machines and that they were generally accompanied by a massive drop in temperature.

I also had one report from Andrew, one of the night shift bag machine operators, that he had taken a spirit home with him and that his wife and kids were being pestered by similar things which were happening at the factory and that one evening his wife was actually taking a bath when an orange-tinted face materialised in the bathroom. The temperature dropped and the face melted away into the outside wall.

Andrew, incidentally, lived near to the factory, probably no more than a quarter of a mile up the hill.

I also began to hear stories about the service tunnels. These were underground tunnels which apparently ran around the site connecting various substations together. In other words, heavy power cables could be run underground to a particular substation without excavation work being required. Now it seems that the tunnel feeding our substation, which was situated to the far left centre of the warehouse, was reputed to be haunted and that the site electricians would not enter the tunnel for a king's ransom. It was also said that in years gone by the village had a coven of witches and that they would hold rituals in the tunnel or its vicinity. How true this was I don't know, but I intend to research it someday.

In fact there were many rumours which circulated but I am trying to keep well to the facts of what I witnessed myself. We were well into autumn now but the weather seemed strangely warm for the time of year. I can remember one of these warm autumn days in particular; it was Sunday and even though I got very few days off I had decided to call in at the factory to make sure everything was alright.

I arrived late morning around eleven o' clock, and as I pulled up in the front yard I spotted Thomas the duty extruder operator sat on the low wall outside the loading bay personnel door, he was smoking a cigarette and holding a large pot of tea.

On my arrival at the door Thomas extinguished the cigarette with the sole of his boot, and invited me to 'Come and check this out mate'. Whatever did he mean, I wondered as he led me into the factory.

As I entered the factory it seemed dark, having come inside quickly out of bright sunlight, but what hit me was the very strong smell of oily wool, a smell which you would expect to encounter if you entered a textile mill.

Thomas went on to tell me that the smell had been there throughout the factory all morning ever since he came in on shift. He had also noticed small shining balls of light floating around the place roughly eight feet from the ground, also a dark grey shape of a man stood by the bottom fire door, but the figure melted away as Thomas walked bravely towards it, only to be replaced by a drop in temperature, a strange small grey cloud and an awful pungent rotting smell.

Having said that, there had been no more apparitions since the figure had melted away an hour previous to my arrival, but the smell of cloth and textiles had persisted along with noises of unseen children laughing and the sound of heavy wooden carts being dragged around, in fact things which many of us had witnessed on many occasions.

The two of us decided to share some cake that Thomas had brought in to finish off his lunch and I made myself a coffee in the canteen, but on emerging from the canteen holding my coffee and cake with the intention of eating it in the sunshine I noticed the smell of wool had disappeared and the atmosphere was back to the usual polythene smell.

'Well,' said Thomas, 'it's as if they were waiting for you to come, to let you witness what I had experienced.' Maybe he was right!

3 CHRISTMAS AT THE FACTORY

December soon arrived and, before we knew it, Christmas was upon us. Christmas, as I mentioned earlier, was the only time in the whole year that we shut down the machines.

Everyone took a well-deserved holiday which lasted for two whole weeks, thus taking in New Year. Everyone, that is, except me and the two engineers who worked for us performing regular maintenance. It was our duty during this festive season to carry out the essential maintenance to the machines, thus ensuring the reduction of costly repairs in the following year.

We worked most of the days available during that two-week window, changing filters, replacing carbon brushes, oil changes, new replacement bearings, in fact all manner of engineering work that needed to be done, and to be honest we even worked until the late afternoon of New Year's Eve. Well, at last, that afternoon around three o' clock the last oil change had been completed and the three of us made our way down to the lower warehouse, where we had a small workshop which doubled up as a changing room.

As the two engineers who had been assisting me were eagerly getting changed and chatting about the forthcoming New Year's Eve festivities, I found myself peering down one of the aisles, which ran for approximately 100 feet and was lined with fifteen-foot-high racking, which ran the full length, and on both sides of the aisle.

I had for a moment thought I had seen a dark figure move between a few of the pallets of bulk cardboard boxes which were stored somewhere near the far wall. I was just about to point out to the two lads what I had just seen, or thought I had seen, when it occurred to me that I would not want to spoil their jubilant afternoon. After all, they were looking forward to a good night out and then a couple of days away from the factory, and dear me, they deserved it. Between us we had serviced just about every machine in the place and that included all three air compressors.

'Well,' I called out, 'that's it, boys. Let's lock up and get out, and at least we have managed to get all the work done without a single psychic experience.'

I had hardly got the last word out of my mouth when, starting from the far end of the racking, 100 feet away from us, a pallet fell down from the racking. It fell from a height of nine feet and it appeared to be thrown off the racking into the aisle, then one by one down the whole length of the racking every pallet which was stored on the nine-foot shelving also threw itself. The three of us stared in amazement; it was impossible what had just occurred but we had all seen it happen. We quietly walked the length of the factory, extinguished the lights, locked up and went home.

The next day was New Year's Day. I was treated to a lie-in, and breakfast in bed by my wife. While she was serving the bacon, eggs and coffee I found myself relating the story of the previous day to her.

'Yes,' I explained, 'those pallets came down one by one; some of them had up to 700 kilos of finished goods on them; there's a heck of a mess to sort out and do you know,' I went on, 'the pallets weren't connected to each other in any way whatsoever. There was at least twelve inches between them so it could not be caused by the domino effect, no, whatever did this pushed each one individually.'

Before Tammy could answer me, the phone rang. It was Andrew, one of the night shift operators, in fact the one that I mentioned lived just up the road near to the factory.

He told me that he had just walked down the hill from his house to call at a friend's home, and whilst passing our factory had noticed a pool of water coming into the yard from under the loading bay door. Obviously either a tap had been left on or we had suffered a burst.

I hurriedly finished the wonderful full English breakfast that my wife had prepared for me whilst dressing myself at the same time. Then it was down to the car and away, my thinking being that the quicker I got to the factory the less damage would be caused. After all, the last water burst we had suffered some months previously had been in the warehouse, and ended up costing us hundreds of pounds in damage to two pallets of cardboard boxes. I did not want a repeat of that.

It was a twenty-minute drive from my house to the factory but by the time I had arrived, the water from the burst was trickling under the loading bay door and into our front yard area; in fact a small stream of water was right across the yard and had begun to run down the main road, next to the wall.

As I fumbled for the factory keys, a voice called out. It was Ronnie, the works engineer from the factory above ours, that is to say the next factory up the hill which was on a higher level by about five feet. He jumped over the wall and accompanied me into the factory to survey the damage. Luckily there was no damage at all, the water had entered our factory at a height of five feet, through the dividing wall of our two premises, part way up the wooden staircase which led to the overhead office. The escaping water had then run along the floor past the toilets and canteen area then under the roller shutter door into the yard, in fact not coming into contact with anything that could be damaged.

I asked Ronnie what had caused the burst and he invited me to come up to his factory to both have a cup of tea and to inspect the sprinkler head which had fractured, causing the damage and resulting leak.

On arrival in the higher building I could see that we had been lucky not to suffer any damage as Ronnie's finished goods area had taken a fair soaking from the aerial deluge from the sprinkler. The water must have been raining down for at least a couple of hours as the place was saturated and by the looks of it would have to be an insurance claim, judging by the amount of water damage to at least twelve pallets of product.

Ronnie, however, went on to tell me that the burst was not his main concern, and that he had ordered a new sprinkler head to be fitted by the five engineers, who were on their way even though it was New Year's Day, and he would then leave the factory heating on to avoid any further risk of frost damage.

No, his main concern, I learned while sipping the hot drink he had made for me, was a strange tale of what had happened as he had become aware of the water burst.

Apparently he had been on an early morning routine visit to the factory. It had been closed for Christmas since the twenty-second of December and wasn't due to open until the second of January. He therefore had made a habit of calling in every morning to make sure that all was in order, and so it had been every day through Christmas until this morning when he had discovered the leak.

Ronnie had, however, this particular morning brought his seven-year-old boy with him as his wife had been left in bed for a lie-in following the New Year's Eve celebrations they had enjoyed the previous night.

On entering the factory and discovering the burst, Ronnie had led his son into the office while he went off to isolate the water pipe supplying the sprinklers. Upon returning to the office he found his son staring up the long alley between the pallets.

'What are you looking at?' enquired Ronnie.

His son pointed up the alley and asked, 'Who is that strange-looking man, Dad?'

Ronnie stared up the dimly lit alleyway but could see nothing, finally walking its distance and back. 'There's no-one there, son,' Ronnie assured his son.

'Yes there is; you walked right through him,' was the answer.

Ronnie shivered and took his son into the office. 'Can you draw me a picture of the man?' he asked.

While Ronnie was on the phone arranging the engineers to make emergency repairs to the sprinklers, his son was busy drawing a careful picture of the figure he reckoned was still there amongst the pallets, and when eventually Ronnie came off the phone and looked at the face the lad had drawn he gasped.

'Well that's not at all right is it, one eye on the left is in the usual place in line with the bridge of the nose but the right eye is down by his chin.'

The seven-year-old agreed, telling Ronnie, 'That is how his face is and he is bleeding from the lower eye.'

Ronnie panicked and took his son home, not quite understanding what was being seen but suddenly starting to have an awful feeling that there was indeed something lurking there that did not want to be viewed by an adult.

It was a few days later, when I was relating this story to a chap who had called at the factory with his wife to buy some bin liners. Apparently he had worked in this particular part of the factory when it had been used by the previous manufacturer, and on listening to my recollection of Ronnie's tale, the man told me that the area where the young lad had seen the strange figure had been the bar store and that he had heard a story of one of the workers in the bar store being hit by a falling length of iron bar which had been stored on high racking, and that it had come down point first, skewering the unfortunate man through the skull. Well that would involve your eye, wouldn't it?

He also told me that he would return some day and give me a few hours of tales of strange things that used to happen while he was working at the factory, but he never kept that promise and I never saw the chap again.

Now then, Michael I think we are getting near our refreshment target of Hereford, but I think I have just time to relate the most strange of all the happenings that I experienced at the factory.

It was early January and the factory was settling back into its normal production routine, the mess caused by the fallen pallets had been cleaned up and I had now started working again on permanent day shift doing my normal job of running the factory, planning the production and controlling the staff.

I had a fairly rigid routine, and had to keep to it due to the high level of orders that had to be manufactured and delivered. Besides coordinating the extrusion and then conversion, or bag machine production, I had to make sure transport was organised for finished goods delivery, and that the correct polymer, boxes and labels were in stock.

I kept a day book of new and complicated orders, updating it through the course of the day. I had also taken to leaving the factory at around 7pm after the evening shift had got settled in, and usually after the last delivery wagon had left the site. I had also got into the habit of stopping off at my local pub on the way home. The pub was called the Royal and was handy for my house, being only half a mile up the road, and although being popular it was usually quiet during the time that I called in the early evening.

I would stick to a routine of just one pint of beer, and whilst sipping the drink over the course of perhaps half an hour I would read through my day book and update it as necessary, making a plan for the following day's production. Then it would be just a short drive before arriving home for a hot meal and bit of family life.

It was my first call of the new year at the Royal; I drew up outside, got out of my car, taking care to lock it, and then strolled into the lounge bar. I ordered my usual pint of bitter together with a bag of salted nuts and made myself comfortable near to the open log fire that was crackling away in the hearth. I took out the day book that was my constant companion with the intention of updating it, but froze when I heard a voice in my ear a deep, warm unseen voice.

'Alf, oooo Alf,' it said.

I was in shock. It was the same voice I had heard weeks earlier in the toilets at the factory. I stood up without even taking one drink from my glass, I picked up the day book and my briefcase and left the pub.

As I approached my car which was parked just outside the Royal I noticed that the headlights and tail lights were on, not only that but the courtesy lights inside the car were also turned on. I knew that I had not left my lights on and besides that the courtesy lights have to be physically switched on, and why would I do that? I unlocked the car door, turned off the courtesy lights and drove home.

On arriving home I unlocked the door, came into the hall, put down my briefcase and made sure I had locked the door behind me, then upon entering the lounge, I put on my usual smile enquiring what was for dinner, choosing not to mention to Tammy what had just occurred.

I remember the stew and dumplings being amongst the best I had tasted for some time, but could not get the voice in my ear out of my thoughts. After dinner I sat on the couch with the intention of watching a bit of TV.

'Where's the remote?' I asked Tammy. Well, it had gone. We searched high and low but could not find it. It was while we were looking for the remote that we both heard a very loud banging from the hall. I immediately thought that someone must be trying to get in as I knew definitely that I had locked the door, but on arriving in the hall, the banging stopped and, as I expected, the door was locked and secure. The only sign of movement of anything was that my briefcase was lying in the middle of the hall face down, nowhere near where I had left it.

A thought ran through my head, 'I bet the missing remote is in my briefcase.' I gingerly unlocked the briefcase and opened the lid, well, there was no remote in there but all my paperwork and documents were ripped into shreds. Unbelievable!

I unlocked the outside door and slowly opened it, peering out into the darkness, and as I did so, our little black pet cat ran out of the house with its fur on end, making a sharp meowing sound as it disappeared into the small wood on the far side of the road.

This was turning into a really strange night. Tammy and I stayed at the door calling out, hoping our pet cat would return, but to no avail. It had gone, but what had frightened the poor little thing?

I resolved to still stay quiet about the pub incident as we locked the front door and re-entered the lounge, but imagine our surprise when laid in front of the television on the hearth rug was the missing remote, and what was even more surprising was that there beside it was my wife's engagement ring which had gone missing from the bathroom several weeks previously.

Tammy had taken the ring off to have a bath one Saturday morning while she was alone in the house and on getting dressed had discovered it to be missing. It was strange because the ring had been next to her wedding ring which was still where it had been left, on the window sill. No amount of searching had found the ring and now it had appeared as if by magic next to the TV remote.

The next day was rather uneventful, but I did find time to make a phone call to the local church minister and arranged a meeting with him to discuss the strange haunting. He promised to call me before the end of the week with a date for a definite visit to our factory.

In the evening I managed to get away an hour early, deciding to visit my mother who I had not been able to see for a good week due to the pressure of work.

I arrived at mother's cosy but small cottage around six-thirty; she was overjoyed to see me, as she always was. The kettle was soon on and a plate of biscuits was brought out.

'Alf,' she said, pouring the coffee, 'you will not believe what happened here last night, it's really shook me up and I can't explain it.'

I sat down with my coffee and listened to her talk; I was amazed. Apparently she had been sat down resting for a good hour after having had her evening meal watching the television when she caught sight out of the corner of her eye some movement behind the television stand. She rose from her seat to investigate and was surprised to see a small black cat jump out from behind the TV stand. It ran silently across the lounge, and leapt onto the window sill behind the long heavy curtains which my mother had closed some time earlier. She then cautiously opened the curtains expecting to reveal the little black cat sitting on the window sill, but to her surprise there was no cat to be found. It had simply disappeared.

It could not have jumped down without being seen, and come to think of it, if the cat had tried to jump down it would have had to disturb the curtains, which had not moved at all.

Luckily both doors of the sitting room were closed as this was all taking place. So my mother knew that the cat had to be still in the room and so began a search of the room but to no avail, the search had proved fruitless, and therefore she came to the conclusion that it must be her mind playing tricks.

I sipped my coffee, listening intently to this bewildering story Mother was telling me, but I was putting two and two together.

'Mother, I can tell you exactly the time that you saw the little black cat jump onto your windowsill, it was seven forty-five, am I right?'

Mother thought for a minute and then, looking puzzled, nodded and went on to confirm that it was indeed the time she first spotted the cat, she was sure because the break had just started as she watched 'Coronation Street' on the TV.

I then ran through the previous night's events with Mother, trying not to miss out any of any of the details, but pointed out that the moment our little black cat ran terrified from the house was the exact time that she had first seen it appear in her cottage. We both concluded that the events were somehow connected, but in any event the cat was never again seen, neither at my Mother's house nor ours.

During the following few days, I decided it was time to ask for help. After all we had lost several good workers, who were too afraid to come to the factory, the strange goings on were showing no signs of abating and on top of that, whatever it was seemed to be attaching itself to me.

4 THE EXORCISM

I eventually again contacted the local vicar, and had a rather long telephone conversation with him outlining some of the more troublesome events which had taken place, and I remember thinking at the time that he seemed to have some knowledge of the things I was referring to.

Within a few days plans were in position for an exorcism of the factory. The exorcism would be conducted by a Catholic priest, who I believe was well versed in such matters, and the Anglican vicar who I had first spoken to. The staff were asked to attend if possible and a time was set for 6pm on the following Wednesday. We all waited excitedly for this exorcism, hoping that it would bring an end to the nightmare of ghostly goings on, which most of us were being made to endure.

The day arrived, and finally the two holy men with whom our hopes rested were sat in the office along with myself and a large proportion of the staff. Only the extruder machines were left running because, as I pointed out earlier, they can't be turned on and off easily so one of the extruder staff had to miss the office meeting, but apart from Steven we all listened intently to what the priest had to say.

For around about an hour, everyone was given a chance to speak, recalling their own particular experiences but not referring to any hearsay; in other words it was hoped that only genuine informatics were to be considered. I along with the others had my chance to relate as many incidents as possible and I noticed during the whole time we were speaking or indeed discussing certain similarities in our statements that the priest was taking notes.

Eventually, however, the main of the stories had been told, tea and biscuits were served and it was then down to the two priests to give their opinion of our situation.

The Catholic priest spoke for the two of them and seemed to take the lead. He went on to say that we seemed to have two things going on here. The first was a place memory. A place memory, he went on, was fairly common in situations such as ours, and although no-one has yet been able to ascertain why. It seems that some old buildings seem to act as a tape recorder, recording events which have happened in times long gone, then certain present-day movements could cause the 'recorder' to play back happenings of times past. These could take the form of sounds such as we had heard, of children talking, or carts being moved about, sometimes glimpses of shapes or figures from the past and more rarely the smell of a previous age. This is briefly and broadly a place memory, although the subject is far broader in reality.

The second thing that was apparent was that we had a poltergeist; this was causing objects to move sometimes slightly, and unseen, just playfully moving things about, or sometimes moving large objects such as the extruder reel bar that had catapulted itself several feet. It could even be blamed for the vicious drumming on the metal dividing wall between the two factory units; again poltergeist activity is a big subject and time did not allow further expansion but he did point out that such activity is usually associated with one of the victims of the experiences and hinted that he thought it was I that was attracting this poltergeist attention. The meeting at this point was concluded and the ritual of exorcism was now to take place. We all paraded down the wooden staircase which led from the office down to the factory floor. We continued to the middle of our production unit where the priest held a small ceremony which included prayer and lots of Latin speaking; he all the time was scattering holy water and blessing machines or areas.

We walked behind him, stopping to bless, chant and spread holy water through all parts of the factory and warehouse, eventually arriving at the back personnel door at the far end of the factory by the bottom extruder.

A longer final Latin prayer was said here, and I noticed as the priest was running through what seemed to me the concluding part of the exorcism, the temperature dropped, in fact it plummeted. I felt frozen and to say we were standing amongst such heat-intensive machines it was absolutely unbelievable how cold I felt. Then as the priest gave the final blessing accompanied by the sign of the cross, the air temperature immediately returned to normal.

Everything now felt good, there was a strange settled feeling in the place, as we all strolled back the length of the building to the canteen, chatting amongst ourselves and listening to the friendly hum of the extruder machines. I instructed the staff to have a free coffee from the drinks machine on me and take a fifteen-minute break whilst I saw our two saviours safely back to their car.

I opened the pass door which was situated between the front yard loading bay door and the canteen to let the two priests out, and whilst chatting on the short distance to their car the Anglican priest confirmed to me that in times past this had been the original Silks Mill, which had been a very large and busy woollen textile mill. Now obviously many of the old buildings had been altered or even replaced, but he went on to say that, in his opinion, the place memory voices we had heard may be a throwback to that time in history. After all, child labour and wooden carts were common in those days.

As they left and I turned to return to my staff I made myself a promise that one day after I retired I would make it my business to research the history of this building and try to make some sense of what I had witnessed over the last twelve months.

On entering the building I was greeted by the night shift extruder operator who had just come on shift and taken over from Steven, whilst I had been chatting with our two now-departed guests.

'Well, maybe I hear that I am in for a peaceful night for once,' he smiled, 'Steven has told me all about the exorcism.'

As Thomas was brewing a large pot of tea in the canteen I gave him a quick rundown on what had occurred that evening and accompanied it with an assurance that he would no longer be troubled by our unwanted spirits. I also remember mentioning to the evening shift staff who were preparing to go home shortly after that I had noticed a massive drop in temperature at the conclusion of the service and, to my astonishment, they spoke of having the same experience. Yes, at the final blessing we all felt the temperature drop and also felt its return to normal at the same time; it just proved to us that there were indeed forces of which we had little knowledge at work.

Ten o' clock arrived quickly that day it seemed; the evening shift left, in high spirits – excuse the pun. Then I ran through the night's production requirements with the night staff. I felt terribly exhausted, but then, it had been a long eventful day. No time for a beer tonight, just home, supper and bed, I thought to myself, putting on my overcoat. I strolled down the production shed to alert everyone that I was going home, when suddenly I felt the temperature begin to drop. It shot down quickly and I realised that I wasn't the only one to notice; Thomas the extruder operator was looking anxiously towards me and the two bag machine operators had stopped their machines to don their jackets.

In almost an instant before I had time to think, the freezing air was accompanied by a tremendous banging on the steel dividing wall. It went on and on. We heard what appeared to sound like a human voice shrieking; the lights flickered and dimmed. It was horrific: the atmosphere felt evil. This was the worst thing any of us had witnessed so far; it was as if something had watched the evening's attempts to cleanse the place by means of exorcism and decided to show us in no uncertain terms that we had failed. Perhaps whatever we were dealing with did not want to go to rest.

The noise stopped, the temperature rose and the lights returned to normal. The four of us stood looking at each other silently with the background hum of the extruder machines the only thing to break the forced silence.

I stayed at the factory until eleven o' clock, by which time things seemed to have nervously returned to some form of normality. I said my goodbyes, but I must admit that night I had mixed feelings, on the one hand glad to be away from the place but on the other I felt bad leaving the three workers to the impending night.

Other the following three months, nothing changed at the factory. In fact it became apparent that the exorcism had been a complete waste of time; it was as if whatever it was found it somehow amusing and probably considered that it had won. Several of the staff left, I suspect they had just had enough of the place and amongst the leavers was myself. My business partner and I, for whom I had, and still have, a high regard, decided to go our separate ways. Thinking back now, I believe had it not been for the ghostly goings on that we would have remained in business together; anyway for whatever reason we parted company.
I did have cause, however, to return to the factory several weeks after my leaving, to sort out some financial matters which had to be dealt with by my ex-partner's wife.

It was a late spring afternoon, I remember driving into the front yard and letting myself in through the pass door. Jane was standing just outside the canteen door holding a coffee, she seemed glad to see me and we chattered for quite a while before going upstairs to the office to conclude our financial business. We then said the usual farewells and began to descend the wooden staircase which led down to the factory floor; it was then that Jane remembered something and stopped me leaving the factory.

'Alf,' she said, 'can you remember the first time you saw an apparition, where was it, can you recall?'

Of course I could recall that day, it was an orange shape, sort of like a figure with no features and it appeared for a short time right at the bottom of the wooden stairs that we had just descended.

Jane bent down and pulled away the thin, worn but large woollen mat that was laid at the bottom of the stairs then pointed to a faint inscription which was carved into the stone floor. It read RIP then a name and date which I now can't recall. I felt a shiver run down my spine, but after all that had gone on I felt no surprise to be shown this.

Just as I was concluding what I considered the comprehensive compilation of the factory sagas, we passed to Welcome to Hereford sign.

'We need a rest, Michael and I know just where to go for a good meal and a rest; it's the perfect place to refresh ourselves, eat, and plan the final leg of the journey to Fishguard.'

It was only a matter of ten minutes until we found ourselves sitting in the lounge bar of the Priory Hotel, a rather imposing building nestled amongst some beautiful gardens and small buildings with an old graveyard to its right-hand side which constituted one of the lawned seating areas. Yes, this place had character and in some way encouraged me to continue with the story whilst we dined and later rested before starting off once more with Fishguard to target.

The food we were served was something else, absolutely the best home cooked food. We had selected the steak and ale pie with new potatoes; it had been served with green vegetables from their own garden. This wonderful meal was washed down with a glass of local scrumpy and followed by a simple vanilla ice cream topped with grated mint chocolate.

While we were enjoying our meal and for a short time after, I took the opportunity to recap my story so far.

If you remember, Michael, the purpose of accompanying you on your journey to Fishguard was to help ease your mind as to the reasons that we are all on Earth and the spiritual expectations of us all. I earlier pointed out to you that during the majority of my life so far I have been terribly lucky to have had many supernatural experiences, and had also had the benefit of the recollections of my mother, who it seems was also gifted with spiritual sight and understanding just as I consider myself to be.

The only way that I could sensibly tell my story was to start part way through my life, in fact at a point in my late forties when, whilst running my own business in an old factory building manufacturing polythene bags, I had the good fortune to witness a myriad of supernatural events.

It was these events and then the twelve months of psychic goings on which affected the lives of me and my staff that led me to reflect back to my early childhood, piecing together the figures of spiritual evidence, thus leading me to the answers to all the great questions that we all ask and think about, concerning our existence and purpose of us being on this Earth.

So as not to waste any time Michael, bearing in mind that the next leg of the journey to Fishguard will be my last chance to complete my story before you sail for Ireland, I will quickly fill you in on the events which occurred following my departure from the factory and the Yorkshire village.

I must say it was in some ways a relief to be away from the spooky factory although I must admit I did miss the staff and also the busy day-to-day workload which I seemed to thrive on. But it wasn't long before another equally demanding job came my way, and it was during this next period of time that I had the very good fortune to meet you, Michael, and your lovely family.

The job opportunity I am referring to was a position in a newly formed polythene bag and recycling company in the Republic of Ireland. It was at a chance meeting that I was introduced to an Irish businessman who had got involved in our field of work.

The company he ran were looking for someone with my extensive background of both the polythene and engineering business, so as to modernise the existing factory and create a new product range. Needless to say, I jumped at this opportunity and it was only a matter of weeks before I and my family had relocated to Ireland.

The factory was a modern building with several offices, in a very rural area of Eire. In fact it was so rural there was no mains water, therefore water had to be pumped from underground. The machinery, however, was pretty good, so to look at the overall situation there did not seem to be much to stop me developing the range of polythene that the owners required.

My family were given use of a country cottage; it was a fairly old cottage but had been tastefully modernised. Again, there was no mains water so the well at the back of the place had been fitted with an electric pump to make things easier.

It was a fairly spacious cottage with wonderful views, it had an open fire and there was a good stock of logs in the small outbuilding which also housed the water pump.

Over the next few weeks I got very involved in the factory, working late most evenings, just as I had done in Yorkshire, but it was always a pleasure to return home, and no matter what time I got back there was always a meal and a smile waiting for me from my wife.

But things started to get a little weird. I noticed that

practically every night when we went to bed, that within a minute of two of pulling up the blankets I would start to have visions.

These visions were very strange: my eyes could be closed or open but in the dark I would see floating before me faces. They were faces of men, from the shoulders upward; they would drift from left to right at, I guess, six feet from me, as one face moved to the right another would replace it. This show would go on for several minutes and then they would fade away until the following night when the whole thing would repeat itself.

During the days that followed these 'sightings' began to feel very disturbing, especially having experienced so much back in England. I thought long and hard about the faces and realised that they were always wearing strange hats, sometimes with the odd feather in the hat. They reminded me of what we would imagine the Cavaliers to look like during the time of Cromwell: most of the figures had a moustache, some even had a small beard and the odd one appeared to have a very large collar, also associated with Cavalier types.

On one particular night in late autumn I retired to bed expecting the face parade but dropped off to sleep almost immediately, thus missing the usual entertainment. But I woke with a start. I felt myself to be drifting, for a moment I thought I was dreaming, but I stared through the crack in the curtains to see the moon shining through the window and the same familiar objects around the room. No, I was sure that I was awake, but what was this drifting feeling? It was as if I were floating through the air, yet I was still in bed. Then the whole room changed, and although I was lying in my bed I felt that I was also walking.

I walked through a low wooden door made of old brown vertical thick planks, then up about twelve wooden creaking steps. At this point I remember looking down and seeing that I was wearing leather boots that went from toe to up past my knees; they were brown and shiny, I remember. As I reached the top of the steps I entered a low room about twelve feet wide by thirty feet long. I had to dip my head to get under the long roof beam at the top of the staircase. On looking into the room I saw five long wooden tables with several rough-looking men sitting around the tables drinking ale from what looked to be mugs made of wood, and a rather short but well-built serving wench wearing a long blue dress with a white shawl about her face and shoulders, serving beer from a heavy wooden tray.

I moved towards the window which was made of very thick glass made up of many small panes, some of which were missing. I peered out through the hole which was there courtesy of the missing panes and saw a strange sight. It was a tree, a really big oak tree: the trunk of this tree would, at a guess, be a good three feet in diameter; the trunk then came above ground level approximately three feet before splitting into two trees growing from the one trunk. It towered high into the sky, in fact I could not see the top, but whilst I stared skyward attempting to see the top of the enormous tree I saw both trees catch fire from the sky and proceed to burn down to the ground, in fact back to the single trunk that had supported the pair of enormous trees.

As my eyes lowered to the trunk of the tree I saw a brass plate nailed there. It had an inscription which simply read RIP. I turned back towards the strange inn to find nothing: I was back in my bed just as I would normally be at this time. A watery moon lit up just enough for me to know that I was at home in bed and all was well.

The morning came and I awoke with the previous night's experience fresh in my mind, I remember feeling terribly uneasy, but on relating the story to my wife she told me to forget about it, and after all that we experienced in England it was probably just my imagination playing tricks. Anyway she hoped it was so; it's the last thing we need for all that to start up again, especially as we were beginning to feel so settled and relaxed at last. I hesitatingly agreed with Tammy, in some ways feeling rather foolish for making a drama out of what could be just a silly dream and set off to the factory to face a new day at work.

I soon found myself as busy as I ever had been. The orders for our new product range were rolling in, the staff were working flat out and yet another new machine had been ordered to keep up to the expansion program. The time got to 11am and I was just thinking that a cup of tea with a sandwich was the next priority when the phone rang for me.

I answered it to find it was Tammy who excitedly asked me, 'Have you heard the news?' 'No,' I replied, 'this factory is nowhere near any communication, the only news I get is when I come home at night.'

'Your dream, it's come true,' she blurted out, 'your dream of the burning tree.'

I asked her to slow down; how could a burning tree be on the news?

Over the next few minutes she proceeded to explain to me that the twin towers in America had been attacked that morning and that they were burning from the top down, also people were dying. 'Don't you see the connection,' she went on, 'the twin towers and the twin trees, the sign RIP?'

I felt shocked; it seemed to fit. I saw this in a vision, hours before it happened.

I did not remain much longer in Ireland; things don't always work out how you want them to, but as I said earlier at least I met you and your family, Michael. We shared many a good Saturday night at the country club and have remained best friends ever since.

As I say, Michael, things don't always work out, and this seemed to me the way my life had always been, moving from job to job but never quite getting to the peak. I always seemed to be working hard but the luck side of things never seemed to run with me. But on returning to England it seemed that things were about to change. I bought a house very near to a house that I had previously owned when I was married to my first wife, and was very lucky to buy the house very cheaply, probably the reason being that the old couple that had lived in the house had allowed it to fall into disrepair.

The new house took a good couple of months for my team of builders to modernise but we were soon settled in and very comfortable. The position of the house suited me also because it was in walking distance of my mother's cottage, only a good ten minutes' walk away.

It wasn't long, however, after settling in that strange things began to happen, small things at first, such as articles going missing then turning up in unusual places; knocking sounds on the internal walls late at night; lights mysteriously being turned on. In fact I could see all the traits of what the old priest had referred to as poltergeist activity and I can't help remembering that he did say it was possible that activity was connected to one of us. I was sure, and had been so for a long time now, that it was me he had been referring to. Was I about to find the same old things starting again? I was about to be answered but in quite a fearful way.

A few days passed. The strange scratching and knocking noises continued but it seemed that only I had noticed anything, so I thought it prudent for Tammy and my son to remain ignorant of what was going on. But on the Thursday of that week Tammy announced that she was taking our boy with her to visit some friends in London and would therefore be away for several days. In a way this suited me as I was in the throes of setting up a new polythene bag manufacturing unit but in a smaller way, in fact what I would call a cottage industry venture.

Tammy duly caught the train the very next morning leaving me to fend for myself. I can remember clearly the first night alone at the new house; I had worked late up at the new factory and bought some fish and chips on my way home. I was starving hungry, not having eaten all day, and by all day I mean a long day. It had got to 10pm, but at least I had achieved my objective: the first extruder was runnable.

After the wonderful meal of fish and chips washed down with several cups of tea I retired to bed knowing that I must be up for 5am to meet a delivery of polymer at seven. But I had barely got into bed when I heard some awfully loud banging sounds on the wall behind the headboard; worryingly the wall was the partition wall to my son's room and I knew there was no-one in there, I was petrified but gingerly crept out of bed and into the adjoining bedroom to find – nothing! I searched the whole house but found nothing, all was quiet.

I returned to bed but slept with one eye open, I can tell you. Then I awoke once more; it was still dark. I fumbled for the alarm clock and checked the time: 2am. As I put the clock back on the dresser I heard clearly three loud knocks on the wardrobe door and at the exact time of the third knock the bedroom light came on. I sat upright for a while before plucking up courage to turn off the light. However on returning to my bed I heard a low groaning sound coming from the area between my bed and the window, but could see nothing. The rest of the night I was constantly roused by bangs, groans and rustling noises, but at 5am I was up and away to work.

The second night that I was to spend alone in the house soon arrived, but I had made up my mind that I would search every bit of the property from cellar to bedrooms, making sure that everything was locked up, thus ensuring that there was no other reason than the supernatural, should any other unexplained noises disturb me during the coming night.

It did not take long, however, before similar goings on

to the previous night began to bother me. There were scratching sounds and knocks both from the wardrobe door and the wall immediately behind my headboard. The staircase light turned itself on and strangely enough my alarm clock sounded off, even though there was still seven hours to go till morning. It was going to be one of those nights but I had made up my mind to tough it out and not respond to this annoyance. But worse was yet to come.

I had managed somehow to fall into a fairly deep sleep in spite of the obvious intended annoyance directed at me, but was awakened at daybreak by a strange greenish aura in the room and a strange sensation that the bed was sloping towards the window. I turned slowly to face the window to see the early morning light shining through the crack in the slightly open curtains. The light mixed softly with the green 'mist', if you can call it that, which I had sensed from waking. Then as my eyes grew accustomed to the darkened room I saw the figure of an old man; he had a gaunt deathly white face, grey hair but with jet-black eyes half closed. He was sitting bolt upright in my bed next to me, staring straight forward, but worse, I realised that he must have weight, for it was that he was causing the mattress to fall to the window side of the bed.

As I struggled to remain calm, the figure, which was dressed in a long striped nightshirt to cover its bony body, simply faded slowly away and as it did so the mattress rose back to its original flat position. The green mist followed his example and melted away, leaving the dawn to break as on a normal day.

Following these two strange disturbed nights, I was happy not to be bothered by whatever it was in such a way again. It had been, it seems, someone or something from the past letting me know it was there, or the old place memory as I had witnessed on earlier occasions.

Over the next few weeks I had in the course of my business become involved with the local Scouts association, who had been offered a lottery grant towards a building project and during my involvement, which was only in the form of helping a friend with a building quotation, I was asked if I could meet a lady from the Scouts Committee to look over some papers. I agreed to this and the venue for the meeting was to be my own house which suited me as all the working drawings were laid out in the dining room.

The lady arrived just after tea the following day and after checking the building drawings and the various contractual papers, I offered the lady a coffee out of courtesy. She agreed to a coffee and began making small talk whilst we drank the coffee I had made. The lady proceeded to inform me that it was a massive coincidence that the meeting should be in this house, because she had been brought up here, and had lived in the house for fifteen years.

She asked me how I liked the house, and I showed her round, pointing out the modernisation that we had carried out since buying the place, which was fairly extensive. I took care not to mention the noises nor my unwelcome night visitor, but as she left, thanking me for the tour and coffee, she turned to ask me:

'Has anything strange happened here since you have moved in?'

I thought hard and then answered her, 'You mean the old man?' She smiled and nodded with a twinkle in her eye, then left without either of us elaborating on the conversation.

It wasn't long before I sold the property; after all with my background of the paranormal and the obvious history in this particular house, I thought it prudent to move along with my wife and son to a more modern home.

I was lucky enough to be able to buy a fairly modern bungalow which was situated fairly near to my old mother's cottage; it was quite large and not very old.

My thinking was twofold: firstly it was unlikely that there would be any psychic presence in a relatively new building and secondly I hoped to be able to convince my mother to move in with us, enabling Tammy and I to better take care of her.

I was quite right in my belief that we should not be bothered by psychic events because as time went on we experienced none at all, but on the second part of my reason for buying the bungalow, that was to entice mother to join us, I in fact hit a stone wall.

Mother insisted that even though she was fairly unwell that she would remain in her cottage along with her memories, small treasures and souvenirs for as long as physically possible. I therefore made it my mission to call in and see her every day, at tea time when finishing work, bringing with me a plate of hot food. I would also call in during the day if I had the chance and spent quite a bit of time with her during weekends, always making sure to bring a bag of welcome shopping with me.

It was during these frequent visits that my mother spent much of her time relating stories and recollections of her early childhood and also the war years, which become an important part later in my story, Michael.

But it was on a particular day I found myself asking Mother for a favour. You have to realise that it wasn't something I normally did as I preferred Mother to rest, but this favour was for a friend of mine.

I asked Mother if she would lay the cards for Tim as I was getting worried about him. He had told me that he was having sleepless nights over his supermarket business in Leeds and could not put his finger on the cause of several problems that had been going on there. These problems were obviously being caused by a member of senior member of staff or worse, it could be a family member; he needed these answers for peace of mind.

My mother, to my surprise, readily agreed. It was a long time ago that I could remember her reading my cards; in fact it was way back, when I split with my first wife. She read them for me and boy, did she get the future right. She told me masses of things which were to come and although I thought at the time that she was telling me what I wanted to hear to console me, I must admit everything she spoke of came to pass. She was a wizard at laying the cards, a gift she had developed with the guidance of her mother in late childhood, she said. In fact we all knew of Mother's prowess as a psychic.

The next evening I brought Tim along to my mother's cottage, where he was welcomed with coffee and plenty of small talk, but it wasn't long before the cards were out and after the usual ritual they were laid. I took a back seat while the proceedings went on and to both mine and Tim's amazement she seemed to pinpoint the cause of his problems in Leeds.

Things did not stop there, though, in fact quite a few other snippets of information were disclosed during the three times that the cards had to be laid. But then came a revelation: she asked Tim on the health of his wife.

'Couldn't be better,' said Tim, Mother, however, insisted he got his wife checked out by a doctor.

Tim agreed, 'Oh, also be careful for your son. He will have an accident but will be OK,' she went on as Tim left the house, clutching the pack of cards that had been given to him for luck.

When we got outside Tim told me that while he was in the house he had an overwhelming feeling of peace, and he was very surprised how accurate she was with what she had spoken about, having never met him before. He also went on to say that he now believed he could sort out his business problem and felt sure none of his family were involved with the problem.

It was a few days later that I received a phone call from Tim, thanking me for the introduction to Mother but also to let me know his son had indeed been involved in an accident and that following his wife's visit to the doctor that she had been admitted to hospital with something fairly serious but that they would be alright and in his wife's case she would be OK because the symptoms were caught early due to my mother's warning.

It wasn't long after this card reading incident that my mother's health worsened; she was taken into hospital where she later died. It was a very sad time for me, but even now I feel her presence with me, guiding me, just as she used to tell me that she was being guided and I am even more convinced now of the gift she and her forefathers were lucky enough to have passed on to me. And this, Michael, is the reason that I feel I must take you back in time to my very early childhood to complete the story, so that in conclusion I will be able to open your eyes to our reason for existence along with the afterlife, in other words what awaits us and how our actions on Earth affect it.

At this point we left the Priory having settled our account, and resumed our journey after topping up the car's virtually empty petrol tank, picking up the road which would take us to Fishguard and Michael's ferry.

As we made our way through Hereford I resumed with the next point of my carefully narrated story.

5 MY LARGEST RECOLLECTIONS

I was born and brought up along with my twin sister in a small village not far from the Yorkshire town of Huddersfield. The year was 1951, not long after the end of World War Two. My father had been serving in the British army throughout the war, fighting mainly in France but finally being posted to Rendsburg in North Germany after the surrender, to keep order along with his regiment. He was to find himself in this pretty but bomb-damaged town until 1948, but during these three years he managed to learn enough of the language to get by and he also managed to find himself a wife, something he, now forty-three years old, had not managed to do back home. His chosen bride (my mother) was called Elfrieda; she was twenty years younger than Dad but the age difference did not seem to bother them. Neither did the nationality difference although they knew deep down that their plan to settle in our village might be looked down upon by the staunch Methodist inhabitants.

However, my mother had been born just over the border of West Germany in Denmark, and technically, although she had been brought up on the German side of the border she was a Dane. So this fact was used when Tom returned to England and introduced her to my grandfather and grandmother with whom he lived in a small stone-built detached house next to the Methodist church and opposite the chapel.

My mother, of course, moved in, and the four of them lived together, but it was only a matter of months before my grandmother died. However it was only to be a threesome for a couple of years until I and my sister were born. I firmly believe that it gave my grandfather a new reason to live when he saw us following his recent loss. I can remember in my early growing up years spending many hours playing with Grandad while Mother was doing the chores and Father was at work.

The first five years, looking back now, were very strange although they seemed normal enough at the time. I have very early recollections of this period; I was probably about three months old when I remember being taken into a wonderful building, our local Methodist church. I vividly recall the day: the sun was shining, glistening on the green marble chippings which covered some of the graves along the sides of the stone path, which led to the massive wooden doors which were the entrance to the church. In particular I recall the gold lettering on a white cross glistening in the sunshine with the heavy green foliage of thick bushes on the roadside railings making a beautiful picture.

As we entered the church through those massive doors, I heard the organ playing and I set my eyes on a burgundy cloth with a gold cross hanging from the pulpit. I remember seeing the water font, then looking across to my sister who was in the arms of my father. We were taken to the font and although I could not possibly know what a christening was, I can actually remember having the sign of the cross put on my forehead by the priest and, believe me, I knew it was a cross. I came away from the font and my sister was treated to the same ritual, the difference being that she cried.

In the months following my baptism I remember having visions of what I can only describe as floating orbs. Every night we would be taken to our cots; my cot was blue and my sister's pink; we would go to bed at about seven o' clock. Our bedroom was quite large and strangely enough I can still remember everything in that room all these years later, the double mahogany wardrobe with the old black hat boxes piled on top, the green, thin, worn carpet with floorboards showing through, the large double bed opposite our cots with my Dad's old army coat laid on it as an extra 'eiderdown'.

And especially the thin curtains which covered both windows: they had flowery patterns, and due to the time we went to bed the sun was still shining through them, so I would stare at the pattern and imagine them to be a story of children dancing and playing. Next to the cots and near to the window was a dressing table with three large mirrors and a large wooden clock which would tick monotonously, I always thought that when I grew up I would not wind my clocks as the ticking keeps you awake.

Anyway, getting back to the orbs, I would as I said have been taken to my cot at about seven o' clock and then probably spent half an hour looking around at my sister, the furniture and the curtains. But as it got more dusky I noticed floating just below the ceiling clouds of tiny coloured bubbles, red ones and green ones, never coming together, sometimes small gatherings of green clouds, sometimes just red, and various sizes of these orb clouds. Very occasionally we got red and green clouds in the same picture. Now the strange thing is that I knew what they were and I had seen them before, to me it was normal even though I was still a tot; I could cast my mind back and remember a time when I myself was a green orb. I was floating amongst bushes I had seen in the churchyard; I was floating amongst other orbs when I somehow teamed up with a red one. I knew at that moment I was to be born. Indeed, I believe I remember before I was born, and along with a red soul the two of us, my sister and I, somehow came from those very clouds of boy and girl 'souls' to be born.

Over my early years I saw the unborn souls quite often floating in green and red and I knew they were the souls of soon-to-be-borns, just like at three months old I knew I had the sign of the cross of the lamb of God on my forehead to protect me and give me everlasting life.

My very early memory was brilliant: I had many recollections from my cot years which were all later verified as being accurate. When I recalled the events in later life my mother would say, 'I can't believe you can remember so well from such an early age.'

There were many incidents I could remember, such as a young girl looking right into our pram. Her face came too close to mine; she was wearing thick round glasses which frightened me more than her stringy yellow hair, partially covered by a multi-coloured knitted cap. I screamed for ages. This incident was quickly followed by a harrowing experience when, whilst being pushed up a rather steep road, the pram caught in some kind of pot hole throwing both me and my sister out onto the pavement, as the pram tipped right over into the road. Thank goodness there weren't many vehicles on the road in those days.

Another powerful recollection I have of those early years was one day the post man delivered a letter just as my mother was about to take us out in the pram. She opened the letter immediately and then burst out crying. My grandfather, trying to console her, asked what was the news and I can vividly remember her sobbing to Granddad that her mother had died and obviously in the time it had taken for the letter to come from Germany, she was already buried.

These, and many other distant memories I have, go to tell me that I was always very aware of what was going on around me. I actually felt that my mind was very finely tuned, but I was a normal child playing with the few toys I had along with my sister, listening to the radio – Mother seemed to have the old Bakelite radio on all day long, while she busied herself with the housework, washing, cooking, cleaning and so on.

Speaking of housework, I remember my favourite. It happened on Saturday nights: it was baking. Mother used to bake cakes for the week; in fact I believe it was the only night of the week that she carried out this wonderful task. After tea she would wash up and then prepare the table with dishes, pans, wooden spoon, scales and many implements. Then would come the flour and baking ingredients. My sister and I would watch in amazement at the goodies being created, but best of all was at the end of the mixing when the cake mixture was heading for the oven, we got to lick out the bowl and the spoons.

All evening as the cakes were being made the radio would be on, usually with a Saturday night mystery being played out or a game show called 'Have A Go Joe'. Sometimes my father and grandfather would go out to the local pub for an hour to partake of a couple of pints and a game of dominoes but they were always back for nine, bringing with them a couple of parcels of fish and chips which we all shared.

It was on these Saturday nights as the fish and chips arrived, the oven was doing its job and we were relaxing after the end of yet another mystery having been solved on the radio, that my mother would tell us of her upbringing in North Germany.

Apparently her grandfather, Helmut, was well renowned for his prophesies and would spend hours in front of the log fire in his favourite arm chair reading his Bible. People came from far and wide to ask for his opinion on matters as it was known that his past prophecies had been uncannily accurate.

My Grandmother also seemed to have a gift, or rather more than one. She was well known as a healer and I have listened to many a tale about her adventures.

One story she told sticks foremost in my mind. The year must have been about 1933: at that time the family were living on the edge of a large forest near Flensburg. Their house was a small detached stone-built cottage with a long front garden and the back of the house backing on to the forest.

On the day of the incident my mother could recall that the two of them, she and my grandmother, had been to the village to buy ham, cheese and bread at the local open-air market. Whilst wandering around the market they had happened upon an old woman dressed completely in black. Her black heavy lace dress flowed right down to her ankles, meeting a pair of muddy black boots; she wore a black shawl and a heavy black headscarf. The old crone tried to strike up a conversation with the pair, enquiring as to the health of Helmut.

My mother remembered how her mother desperately tried not to engage in any conversation, eventually leaving the market in haste and heading home, all the time taking backward glances to make sure they weren't being followed. It wasn't till they were safely back home that Grandma explained to my mother that the old crone was a witch and that she had been responsible for many unhappy events, which, she explained, my mother as yet was not old enough to know about and even if she were, she would not probably find believable, so best left there.

My mother made it her business though to keep insisting on some clarification of the 'events' that were obviously frightening my grandma, as do little nosey girls of seven.

Then all of a sudden there was a knock at the door. My mother looked out of the window and turned in horror to Grandma, 'It's her, it's the crone,' she quaked.

My Grandma moved towards the door, moving Mother out of the way to a safe distance and reached for the door knob.

'Don't open it,' Mother whispered.

But Grandma turned and said, 'Don't worry, she won't come in. Even if I invite her she won't put a foot over the threshold. Watch,' she said, 'I will prove to you she is of

Evil.'

The door was opened and there stood the crone. My mother trembled as she was invited in. 'Thank-you,' said the crone, putting one foot across the threshold. It shot back as if burnt in fire. The crone grimaced and politely declined the invitation to enter; she turned and hobbled away down the path to the road.

'How did you know she would not come in?' enquired my mother, a puzzled look on her face but also a feeling of relief. My Grandma pulled back the draught curtain from the top of the door and there above the door was a cross made from drawing pins, right in the middle.

'You see, the crone did not know of the cross, but she still could not walk under it into the house,' said my grandma. 'Is that not enough proof for you?'

This was a gripping story for me but over the years I found many; another equally captivating tale was concerning the path outside the cottage. My grandma kept chickens and for some time there were losses; a couple would disappear and the feathers would be found along the garden path but never any sign of the thief or indeed the chickens themselves. Helmut, my great grandfather, however, quietly told the family that it was something evil that was targeting our cottage and we must be on our guard, and although this went on right through the summer my grandma suspected it was just a local opportunist taking a free meal.

During the autumn of that year however it was decided that before winter arrived they would have a nice concrete path laid. The workmen duly came, they hand mixed and laid a narrow concrete path which stretched from the front door to the gate by the road. It was done for dusk and everyone looked forward to walking on it the next day, knowing they would not now have muddy shoes every time they walked down to the road through the garden.

Imagine my Grandma's surprise the following day when

she opened the door to find feathers scattered all along her new path. Two more chickens gone, but hey, what's this?

Looking carefully at the newly laid concrete it became clear that impressed into the now hardened surface was a set of footprints or rather a set of hoof prints. Helmut was quickly informed and on the scene.

'Yes, these are cloven hoof prints,' he gasped, 'and not from an animal walking normally; this beast was walking on two legs, its hind legs just like we humans walk.'

The other strange thing was that the trail led up to our door but there was no return trail, but do you know, from that day no chickens were taken again and Helmut left the prints there in the concrete for all to see, never covering them up.

My mother, one winter's evening, told yet another odd tale. It seems that she must have been seven years old and quite settled in to school. In those days there were quite small class sizes, probably no more than twenty; the desks were the old wooden two-child desks, the ones with built-in wooden seats, complete with two inkwells, she added. Now on this particular day in my mother's story a new girl was introduced to the class.

The teacher entered the room holding the hand of the little girl. 'This is Greta, everyone. She is only five but this class is small so she will spend the rest of the term with you. Please help her to settle in.'

Then as the teacher led Greta towards an empty desk, Greta pulled away from the teacher's hand and walked straight over to the desk in which my mother was sitting.

'This is my desk,' she said, 'I want it back. I always used to sit here.' Teacher, try as she might, could not persuade Greta that my mother's desk wasn't hers but Mother ended up having to let Greta take the desk.

The story goes on that Greta's mother was informed as to the misbehaviour and, on coming to school to speak to the teacher, was shocked and upset. It transpired that Greta had a sister who had died at six years old, eight years previously, and had attended the same school and, you guessed it. This had been her sister's desk, but how could Greta have known? My mother was convinced that Greta was the reincarnation of her sister.

Mother was quite sure that reincarnation was only one aspect of life after death and depended largely on circumstance as I will come to later, but she spoke of another similar event which happened the summer following the Greta incident.

Her parents decided that a short summer holiday would be nice; my mother was now eight so they decided to go camping by the river Eider. Along the banks of the river were many quaint villages and they would also have the opportunity to dive for amber. Amber can be found in some German rivers and had a fascination for my mother as her grandma had given her a large piece, complete with an entombed fly, for a present a couple of years previously.

They duly arrived at a village where it had been decided they would camp but when they reached the main street, my mother started to recognise various houses and places. She spoke of people who lived there and where the post office was and yes, that house over there used to be a pub.

Granddad said it was impossible that she could have any knowledge of this village as they had never visited it before, but as Mother insisted and led them round the village accurately telling them what was round the next corner my grandparents became more and more convinced that Mother had been there before and, on enquiring to a local about the house my mother said used to be a pub when she 'lived' here, it was confirmed that the house had indeed been a pub but that it had been converted to a normal house in 1800, 130 years ago. How could she have known?

What was more revealing was that during the camping trip she spoke of a large rock where she somehow recalled playing, and could also remember watching a small boy who looked as if he had gone without both food and a wash for some time, dressed in well patched-up shirt and trousers. He was, as near as Mother could recall, carving letters and a heart into the rock with a small piece of sharpened metal using a large stone as a hammer.

My grandfather upon hearing this account asked Mother to lead him to the spot, and indeed she did so, negotiating the small pathways through the trees, along the riverbank and finally to the rock, which upon inspection was exactly as Mother had described with a worn but still distinct carving etched into the lower part of the boulder at approximately the height you would expect a small boy to be able to work comfortably. Anyhow the carving which had been described by Mother was indeed of a heart, with an inscription which read, Wolfgang-Anna 1776.

It also seemed to me listening to my mother's numerous stories of her early life, of which there are too many to relate in the time we have, it pointed clearly to the fact that my grandmother had, amongst other gifts, the power of healing. This was borne out by one particularly strange account that she recalled, which happened in around 1937.

Early one evening just as dusk was falling, Mother recalled there being a loud, desperate knocking on the heavy wooden front door, and upon my grandmother gingerly opening the door an equally desperate elderly lady had a rapid urgent conversation which led to my mother being taken down to the local hospital along with the two adults.

Mother learned as the three arrived at the hospital that a little girl named Lucy who was in fact the granddaughter of the elderly lady who had desperately knocked on the door, had only hours to live due to coming near to the end of a long illness. It was in fact the hospital doctor who had informed the family, and it had been their decision to call Grandma.

The three of them entered the small side room where

Lucy was laying, very still and ashen, hardly breathing. My mother then recalled the strangest of circumstances. Grandma slipped her hands under the covers, looking towards the ceiling and whispering something which could not be heard, with half closed eyes.

Suddenly without warning the temperature in the room dropped. There appeared to be a strong draught, but the door and window were firmly closed. Grandma stayed fixed in this position for what seemed a good half hour in fact until the draught was felt no more and the temperature lifted. It was at this point that Mother recalled that although there were only the three visitors standing near the bed, that for a few seconds she distinctly saw four shadows on the wall and the fourth was much larger than the two medium shadows and one small shadow.

It was at this point however that the door opened and the doctor appeared. Grandma by this time was sitting down a good couple of yards from Lucy, but to the doctor's and Mother's astonishment Lucy had opened her eyes and regained her colour.

Several days later Mother remembered the elderly lady and Lucy calling at their cottage and that they gave Grandma a very large bunch of flowers.

It was, according to Mother, a good while after this incident that Grandmother was requested on another occasion to help an elderly gentleman who had fallen ill and he was cured fairly quickly following a visit from Grandma. As time went on it became natural to Mother that such things were normal and she witnessed many more equally miraculous recoveries.

Michael seemed to me to be looking rather tired as our car trundled along the motorway crossing into Wales. I decided therefore as we were making such good progress, I would further my story with further information to illustrate the background and connections which eventually bring me to the climax of my tale.

6 PREDICTIONS

'Michael,' I called out, after glancing sideways to realise that my friend was slowly falling asleep, 'please don't drop off now, we're making very good progress and I am sure that we are only a couple of hours away from the ferry port.'

He stirred himself, uttering a whispered 'sorry'. Michael took a drink of orange from one of the bottles of juice that we had brought along. Sitting up, he urged me to please complete that fascinating story as he needed to hear its life-changing consequences before the ferry port was reached.

I quickly resumed my story, but not before reminding Michael that, as I had pointed out earlier, the gift that I seemed to have had been prevalent in my family going back at least three generations and of those, the earliest, which had been my great-grandfather, was, to say the least, one of the most interesting to me.

My great-grandfather's name was Helmut; he had at the time of one of his most prolific prophecies reached old age and spent most of his time inside the house where he lived with his wife and a garden full of chickens.

From morning till night he would spend most of the day reading from the Bible whilst rocking in front of the open log fire. In fact his Bible had probably been virtually committed to memory according to my grandmother, for she could recall him always reading it for as long as she could remember. Yes, she went on, from her earliest memory it was every day he would pick up the book, and as he progressed into old age it seemed to be his only solace.

Helmut was renowned for his ability to be uncannily accurate with his predictions. He was reputed to be possibly the only person in the area who seemed to genuinely have the gift of seeing the future, and for that reason many people would call on him to help them with problems.

Helmut did not, however, embrace this notoriety but over the course of his long life had foretold of many events which did come to pass. My grandma told Mother that some of his predictions were so alarmingly vivid that it seemed to those listening that he was actually there, experiencing the prediction.

Grandma recalled one day, whilst she was visiting her parents near a town called Kiel, Helmut was sitting out in the back garden looking wistfully across his fruit trees which were a mixture of apple and pear, along with a couple of very tall trees which were at that time laden with ripe cherries, signifying that it must have been in the autumn. Her mother came out into the garden with a mug of coffee for Helmut and enquired as to what he was watching.

Helmut pointed to the bottom of the garden, which was about 100 metres to the boundary wall, on the other side of which was miles of dense woodland and said, 'I am watching the huge ships sailing by.' He proceeded to explain that there were many huge battleships and liners sailing in both directions.

'Impossible,' said my grandma and whilst shrugging her shoulders Great-Grandma agreed. But do you know, it was only years later that the Kiel Canal was built and, sure enough, ships did sail exactly where Helmut had seen them.

As the years passed Helmut disclosed much more of his inner thoughts with both Great-Grandma and my grandmother, confiding in them that he found all the answers to life's problems and questions in the pages of his Bible. In fact the Bible has the answers to just about everything we need or want to know; you just have to know how to decode and understand its messages.

This brings me to his most famous prediction. The year was 1938: Helmut was now a very old man, mother was fourteen years old and well able to remember vividly the exact sequence of events that day as she helped prepare the evening meal. It transpired that Grandfather had been made a Captain in the German navy and was to be trained for submarines; this meant better pay and he would be mixing with the elite. Grandma apparently seemed excited but at the same time worried, as war seemed to be looming, so the talk was of 'not to worry, if war comes it will be over soon'.

Helmut suddenly snapped; he had had enough of the talk. He jumped to his feet and brought both hands heavily down onto the supper table, he stared at my grandfather full in the face.

'YES, you know it all don't you?' he snorted. 'You think that because you have landed a plum job in the Navy that you're smart and know it all. Well let me tell you that you know nothing.' He then proceeded to give his most famous ever prophecy.

'You young people, you don't know anything. I tell you now that the war we have just fought and lost is nothing to the war which is about to begin. It's nearly upon us and you talk as if it will be a breeze and will be over in six months. Well I tell you this, this impending war won't be over in six months, more likely six years, millions of people will have to die, many countries will be caught up in it, there will be death and destruction unequalled ever before. That's what you are facing and like the last war Germany will be the losers. I won't be here to see it, thank God, as my time is now short, but take heed that this is not the end, after this second enormous war there is another far bigger war to come, far bigger again than the last two combined.

'It comes early in the second millennium; it starts in the east. Over several years tensions grow, many countries line up in the cold war, many atrocities are committed, the war of words turns into a powder keg, and then! It explodes. Hell looks like a safe haven to what is happening: fire rains incessantly from the sky, terrible never before seen weapons are used, weapons that can kill from outer space, unbelievable carnage, not a country is left out. Millions and millions die from horrific injuries.

'This torment goes on for a full two years until the carnage comes to an abrupt halt and as the smoke and stench of battle subsides those who are left alive have to live with the realisation that they are practically alone in the world. You will walk miles before you come across another human being; nearly everyone is dead. No nation has surrendered, neither has any nation claimed victory. Then and only then will there be peace in this world.'

No one spoke as this respected man walked back to his chair, never repeating to a soul again this prophecy.

I must say that this prophecy sent a chill down my spine, but, as I say, thinking back to when I first heard this tale, I had already seen, heard and witnessed many things of which I was probably of a privileged few who had been privy to such information and insight. It set me off on a sort of quest. I knew that there was a life after death and I had by now gathered from my experiences that how we lived our lives and by what rules, would influence that afterlife.

I had also come to realise that from the orbs to the prophecy, it was all real, all true. I felt so lucky. Now I would be searching even more the age-old questions of where does everything come from; what happens to us when we die; do we have influence over those events? I knew that the answers to these questions were not straightforward, not black or white but they are indeed questions that can be answered and all those years on, Michael, I feel I have learned enough to be able to answer many of them.

Michael, this brings me to the reason I came on this journey with you, I needed to explain to you so you can see as I do that there is hope for many of us, including your parents. But just bear with me while I complete my story. Hopefully we will have time before the ferry sails.

Having negotiated the facts which needed to be explained so far to illustrate the point I am trying to get at, it leaves just one part of my life that I have so far not spoken about, but it is equally important as it provides more evidence to support the conclusions regarding our existence as will once explained become clear.

The period I am referring to is from around the age of twelve through my working life to bring us to the position of where I began my tale. This part of my life, although being the most in years is relatively more sparse of 'events' but nevertheless is part of the story and take only a small amount of time to explain, so bear with me.

When I reached the age of twelve my family moved from the small village where I had been brought up. We moved to a district just three miles from the town centre, quite built up and no longer a rural location.

There were, however, advantages in so far as my father was in walking distance of the textile mill where he worked as a pattern weaver and we, the children, were within walking distance of the high school which was an advantage as there were only streets between me and my friends rather than miles.

There were also disadvantages, the main one being that my grandfather did not want to move and had elected to stay in the village with my uncle and aunt, I did, however, promise him I would visit as often as I could.

Briefly now, so as not to take up too much of the time that we have left before we reach Fishguard. The family had moved to a lovely three-bedroomed modern semi with good gardens. I loved the new school and enjoyed learning. I did keep my word to visit Granddad often and before I knew it, time had flown past and I was leaving school at fifteen years old.

I joined the Yorkshire electricity board as an apprentice and eventually studied power electronics at my own cost. I say at my own cost because that's what it was; the small amount I was earning went towards what I thought would help to give me a work advantage in the future.

During the five years that was spent serving my apprenticeship I worked terribly hard studying for the electrical exams which I was expected to pass whilst working a forty-hour week with the fully trained electricians, and also spending eighty percent of my free time studying power electronics which included building the circuits physically.

The small amount of spare time that I had, I managed to spend with my friends in the various dance halls and discotheques which seemed to be springing up everywhere in the Sixties.

It was at one of these discotheques where I met my first wife. In fact it was her family who owned the place, so it was inevitable that the last twenty percent of my time would be spent there, and we were soon engaged.

The girl who I had first met in the discotheque was to marry me in 1971 but not before I had changed my religion from Methodist to Roman Catholic. This was due to my fiancée being Italian, and to marry in church I was compelled by her family to become a Catholic. This also meant that I had to have godparents who were also Catholics and so two of our friends agreed to fill the positions.

We bought a house quite nearby where I had lived with my mother, father and sister and it wasn't very long before we ourselves were parents to a healthy baby boy.

I was twenty-five now, and had left the Electricity Board; in fact I was working at a large chemical manufacturing company and was employed as an electrician but primarily repairing electronic equipment and instrumentation, which was my dream job. But I realised the job was also a stepping stone, as a vacancy arose for an engineering manager with a polythene manufacturing company, which produced plastic bags.

Polythene bag making was a relatively new industry much in its infancy, but I knew that I had just the right background to make it big in this field. You see, I had, beside a good electrical background, reached a high standard in solid state electronics and had a good knowledge of chemicals, which were the perfect requirements for the highly technically advanced machines, along with the need to understand how the different polymers react using certain production techniques, to make strong polythene bags.

I was enjoying myself in this industry especially when attempting to invent new products by means of blending, altering the machinery to reach the desired requirement. But it was during my first year at the company that the news reached me that Maria, my Catholic godmother had died. It was a shock because she was only thirty-eight years old, and one of the kindest ladies I had ever met.

Being of Italian extraction, a typical large extravagant funeral was planned. She had many friends as well as a large family, so the day of the funeral would be a full day's business, probably going on into the evening.

I was, however, very much tied up in business of my own, attempting to make the best of impressions with the bosses of my new company and because of this, coupled with the fact of not wanting to spend all day at a funeral, I informed my wife only the night before the funeral that she would have to go alone as I had other important business to attend to.

My wife, try as she might, could not convince me to change my mind, in the end agreeing to go alone, but asked me to set the alarm clock for her to five-thirty allowing her plenty of time to get ready. I quickly agreed to this and smartly made my way upstairs to our bedroom. Imagine my surprise when upon picking up the alarm clock I found it already set for five-thirty and the alarm set button had been activated.

I quickly replaced the clock by the bedside, returned to the living room and revealed to my wife that the clock was already set. She swore she had not touched the clock and besides that, it was only during our conversation that she had decided five-thirty would be a good time to get up; normally our clock was set for six-thirty.

Both I and my wife always believed that Maria had somehow set the clock as a sign to me that she wanted me to attend the funeral, and I must say, ever since I have regretted not attending. After all she had attended church to be my godmother when I needed her.

A couple of weeks passed by and the recriminations of my not attending Maria's funeral were dying down, it was becoming old news, when I remember coming home late one Friday night from the factory having had a union problem with the evening engineering staff. We had a late supper and retired for the night.

I fell asleep almost immediately after getting into bed, but awoke with a start somewhere around midnight. I turned to lie on my back and as I did so I was shocked to see a brightly lit face on the ceiling right above me, looking down at me. I nudged my wife and together we stared in disbelief at the face. 'It's Max,' I quaked, as the face faded away, leaving the room again in total darkness.

The next day we did not speak of the strange event which had unfolded during the previous night as my little boy was about and for the fact that Max was a nephew of Maria.

It came as quite a shock, however, when news reached us that Max had died at about the time of us witnessing the strange apparition the previous night and the lad was barely twenty-five years old.

With everything that was going on that spring, it was a breath of fresh air when early summer arrived and it was time to go on our summer holiday. I had booked us a static caravan on a caravan site near Paignton Beach in Devon.

We had stayed at this caravan park once before so knew our way round both the park's amenities and the surrounding area.

On arriving at the camp site we soon got settled in and were quickly re-exploring the place. My son was wide-eyed seeing the clowns outside the club house and whilst the two of us went on to check out the beach, my wife was left to unpack and prepare the caravan.

Evening soon came and after a visit to the cafe for fish and chips it was off to the club house for free entertainment until nine o' clock, then back to the caravan for an early night. After all, it had been a long day if you were to include the six-hour car journey down from Yorkshire.

The caravan had only one double bedroom but the lounge doubled up as a bedroom. My son elected to sleep in the lounge, probably due to the fact that he could watch TV in bed, but at ten-thirty both the TV and light were turned off, followed by instructions to go to sleep; it's a busy day tomorrow.

The following morning, however, I was the first to wake and went to check on my son, enquiring if he had slept well. On speaking with the bright three-year-old I was amazed to hear that he had not slept well.

He asked me, 'Who was that man who was sitting on my bed last night?'

I felt a shiver run down my spine. I told him that he must have been dreaming, but no, my son insisted that a very large man wearing a blue work jacket, brown trousers, a flat cap, hob nailed boots and a silver watch on a chain in his top pocket had asked him some questions. He had asked, 'How is Elfrieda?' and 'Where is your sister?'

I must admit, besides being taken aback by all this I was puzzled. I knew he had experienced something due to the fact that the only person to call my mother Elfrieda was indeed my father who had been dead some years now.

Besides this, the person who was being described to me was indeed my father right down to the silver pocket watch.

To say that I was puzzled was an understatement. I obviously had to believe my son; the information he had given me could only have been gained if my father had actually visited. Besides, my son was only a few months old when Dad died and couldn't possibly have memories of him.

I decided to question my boy further that day and was intrigued to hear further accounts of the conversations that had taken place with our night visitor. Apparently our 'ghost' had also asked about certain other people, so while all this was fresh in our minds, I wrote down the names, which included Dave at Moss, Willie Pole Moor and one or two other equally strange names.

The rest of the week's holiday passed with no further incidents but on returning home I made a point of visiting my mother, not only to bring her the presents that we had bought for her from Devon, but also to relate the visitor tale to her, and to see if she could shed some light on the incident.

Shed light she could. Mother went on to say that her grandson had described his granddad perfectly. As for calling her Elfrieda, I was quite right that only he referred to Mother in that way and always had done since meeting her in Germany all those years ago. And as for the list of names, well they were all old pals of Dad's but had been dead for many years. They carried strange names as my father called them by their first names then added the place where they lived, usually a wild place on the Yorkshire moors, such as Dave from the Moss, or Dave at Moss, as expressed in Yorkshire dialect.

Between ourselves, Mother and I always believed that Dad did indeed visit in the night in Devon and as for his question, where is your sister, well, a girl was born to us the following year, so it seems he was right.

For several years after the Devon incident things returned to normal. The children grew older, I progressed with my company which was bought out by a multinational company and we moved to a bigger house.

It was after we moved to the new house that things went wrong between my wife and me. Our problems resulted in the two of us getting amicably divorced; I did, however, consider myself lucky in so far as I got to keep the children living with me in the family home.

The spilt seemed to make me spend more time than I ever had before with the children, and this brings me to an incident which occurred on Saturday afternoon whilst the three of us were sat in our through lounge watching the TV.

We had just finished a late lunch and were relaxing watching TV, the three of us sat together on our three-seater settee eating our pudding which, if my memory serves me right, happened to be ice cream cornets from the ice cream van – you know, the one that usually arrives before lunch has been eaten. Well, today it had turned up just as we were about to choose pudding and so became a unanimous yes, to savour its delights.

Imagine our surprise when for no reason whatsoever a grey mist began to appear in the room, somewhere near to the corner where the TV stood. It seemed to grow until it resembled a grey cloud, then in a flash it floated the length of our through lounge through the dining area wall and away into the back garden.

We all sat motionless, no longer licking our cornets, which were beginning to drip. The only movement I noticed for two or three minutes was from our cat who, with an arched back, fur standing on end, stared fixedly at the dining room window. The silence was broken by the phone ringing and upon answering it I was given the news that my uncle had just passed away, I told the kids who were distressed at the news, but to this day the three of us believe that the grey cloud was Uncle letting us know that he had passed away.

My mother had very strong convictions and opinions, based upon not only her experiences, but also on the information passed down from our ancestors, most very similar to my own, based on my similar conclusions. One of these convictions was that at the point of death of a human being as a soul leaves the body it can manifest itself in various ways and places. In the case of my uncle I believe this to be true and I believe that the misty cloud was his soul saying farewell.

We had now just arrived at Fishguard, it was early evening and to be honest I had just about had enough of driving.

'Michael, I'm just going to park the car, but I will drop you off at departures so you can organise your ticket. We will meet in the departure restaurant: as I see it, the boat doesn't sail for another four hours in which time we will be able to eat a proper meal, and I will get a decent rest before my return trip to Yorkshire.' He agreed and followed my instructions, not forgetting to phone his brother to arrange being picked up on his arrival in the Republic.

Michael and I duly met in the fairly empty restaurant, we ordered a steak meal with sweet to follow and found a window table overlooking the harbour.

'I don't have much time now, Michael, but I must now quickly come to the conclusions of what I am attempting to tell you, so you eat your meal and don't interrupt me whilst I try to make sense of it all for you. When I've done I feel you will be well equipped to return to your mother knowing that despite her illness and sadness that it is just the beginning of her everlasting happiness.'

Michael began to munch his food, eagerly listening to the rest of my strange tale.

7 FOOTSTEPS OF THE SPIRITS

As I pointed out earlier, Michael, I have by starting at a point late on in my life given you a whole lifetime's worth of events, all of which were needed to show you how I have reached the revelations which I am going to reveal to you now. But the point I would like to begin with is to repeat that it was only when I heard the experiences at my factory that I realised what life and death were all about and had it not been for both my earlier supernatural experiences, coupled with the handed down ancestral information that my mother passed on to me along with her own experiences, I feel that I would not be in the position that I now find myself.

The first message I have to give you, however, is based on the fact that it took me myself until my late forties to realise that material things don't matter, and we all go blindly blundering through life: materialistic, self-centred, not caring for our neighbour – in fact, playing to the gallery, possibly going to church and putting a few bob in the offertory but deep down it's about me, or at best me and mine, not a thought of what is to come, the rainy day, or when we get old, or indeed genuinely, for my neighbour!

If I had not had the experiences to which I refer, I too could have, just as everyone else, gone blindly on to the end and not been in a position as I feel I am in now to use the information to warn others, or as this situation dictates help someone.

I do feel that I must put pen to paper at some stage so that others can share what I have been lucky enough to see, but for the moment it's important that you are armed with my information before you leave for Ireland.

If you cast your mind back to my great-grandfather in Germany, he spent the majority of his time reading his Bible; he used to say that everything is there, all the answers to life's questions along with guidance on how to live our lives. He also pointed out that evil would not go unpunished and as it says in the beatitudes the meek shall inherit the Earth.

This, like a lot of other messages, shouldn't be taken literally as such: it's not saying that all timid people will somehow one day rule the Earth. But we must consider that this earth has many lands, there are many races and religions, each with differing views, but it is my opinion that each religion has its central figure, its God, its focus of worship. I believe that somehow we are all worshipping the same God although we see him through the eyes of each particular religion.

In times gone by some people worshiped the sun; then there were the Roman gods, the Norse gods, the druids with their pagan gods, the ancient Greeks and many more, too many to mention. Many religions were seen over by high priests and the like, but it seems to me these days that the worshiping of the planets has been replaced by a better understanding and a step back from magic and superstition. The arrival of Jesus with his message for mankind and his dying on the Cross for our salvations should steer us all in his ways, but unfortunately it does not. In fact I would go so far as to say most of us do not choose to follow his example and teachings.

It should be everyone's ambition to live a good life, caring for others in the hope of achieving eternal life, but sadly not all our eyes have been opened. It's unfortunate that I don't have time to go into all the details required to make my point clearer, Michael, so I will keep all my points brief in the hope that I touch on enough to get my message across.

The Old Testament was a collection of books which played out the Creation. It told stories of the early world, of Moses and of Holy Wars, but the New Testament depicts the coming of Christ amongst us, and using his apostles his teachings filter out the old ways to show us the path to eternal life.

It's said that there are many worlds throughout the universe which carry intelligent life, but I tell you now, I believe this is not the case. The picture in fact is far simpler than what we seem to believe. This Earth is God's creation and all that he creates is here; he has given us the ability to create further life and the intelligence in his own image to one day understand how to move away and populate his many mansions.

The universe is expanding, world without end; this earth is a selection process, and no, it's not, as some would believe, the way to eternal life to kill in the name of a particular religion to gain eternal reward and happiness. No, that is a misconception: do you really believe that God would create such a beautiful, complicated human being and then allow another human being to kill that creation without taking some form of retribution?

This retribution is not a deliberate form of punishment. No, it's only a consequence, you reap what you sow, you make your own path in life, however you want to phrase it. You can take many quotes from the Bible to easily understand how to live your life to move on to the next part of our eternal existence, enjoying the paradises of far-away mansions.

Just think about it, a person spends his or her life thinking of others, giving what he has both in goods and kindness of heart, caring for children and the sick, not wasting precious time and not speaking ill of anyone. He comes to the end of his life: would it then be fair for his path to take him to the same mansion as another human being who had, for instance, killed other human beings in a twisted idea that this could be what our Creator wanted us to do, or for someone who although blessed with worldly goods died rich, not sharing everything he or she had to give the poor and infirm, or starving children of our world some relief and happiness?

Remember what our Lord taught us, it is easier for a poor man to go through the eye of a needle than for a rich man to enter the Kingdom of Heaven.

Any civilised human being I can guarantee has a good idea of decency, of good and evil. We should not have to be taught that it is a sin to take another person's life.

A human life is sacred, an irreplaceable gift from God. Once lost, impossible to bring back; this statement in itself tells us that under no circumstances have we the right to take life. More important are the murders committed in the name of religion. I must emphasise that, as I have shown, all religions do eventually, however they are worshiped, lead back to the same Creator.

All human beings have exactly the same equal rights in the eyes of our Lord; we are all expected to live in harmony and peace, to share what we have so no-one will starve or live without shelter.

Each branch of every religion, however diverse, must learn to tolerate one another, remembering that we are all governed by the same basic religion, and therefore respect everyone's ways of worship, however diverse.

One day I hope that all religions will come together and worship as one, without the thoughts of conflict between religions and its followers. I also hope and believe that the day will come when wars and conflict will be a thing of the past, but as I have pointed out earlier, it is still away from our reach.

Going back to my second point of the rich man having difficulty in entering the Kingdom of Heaven, remember the story of the poor lady in the temple. She had but one coin in her purse; she put the coin into the offertory box, then the rich man placed several gold coins into the same box for all to see. Jesus asked who had given the most; the answer came back, the rich man of course, but Jesus said no, because the poor lady by putting the one coin into the box gave all she had, therefore giving the most. This brings me to another important point.

With great power comes great responsibility, from both position and wealth. If it was your destiny to be wealthy, no matter how that wealth was gained, it is your responsibility to use the riches not only for your own lifestyle but also to help those less well off, the poor and the needy and the sick.

This applies again to all human beings including all classes, royalty, lords, ladies, bankers, politicians, businessmen and all those who find themselves for whatever reason in an above-average position, which gives them luxury and advantage.

These people must open their eyes and realise that this advantage only lasts for the time they remain on this earth. I have said it before, this world is a place where we all are being tested. We are going through a selection and sorting process of sorts, to put it plainly.

When death finally arrives as it does eventually with all of us, we will have during the time we have enjoyed on Earth already have chosen our path and that path at this point cannot be changed.

The various paths from this life, as I am attempting to point out to you, are all dependent on how we have each lived our lives. For instance, the majority of people who enjoy a position of wealth and power hang on to it, sharing very little. They are greedy self-centred individuals, who spend their lives indulging and showing off what they have to others less fortunate, possibly throwing a few pounds into a charity box to occasionally ease their own conscience, but moreover blocking out the suffering of others that they could, if they had a mind, help to ease.

But the day comes soon enough when they have to leave this life and as the old saying goes, they came with nothing and they go with nothing. But in the majority of their cases, the saying should be, they came with nothing and left with even less, because they have already mapped out the path or route they take after death and I can tell you this with confidence, it is not the one they expect. No, it comes as quite a shock I can tell you. They actually believed that provided that they attended church regularly, gave a few pounds to charity here and there, led a quiet unassuming life and made no ripples, that all would be well at the end.

An elderly gent I used to know once spoke to me of his views of life, he went on to tell me that he had led a frugal life, keeping himself to himself, he had a small family, went to church occasionally, did not drink or swear but eventually hoped to spend the money he had managed to scrimp together on his old age. Well, he died, never having the chance to pamper himself and, do you know, he ended up with the rest of society who are also not prepared to share or care for all humanity. They try to play it safe, lead an unassuming life, steadily building up riches and security, playing the god-fearing game but looking down upon those who have less than them.

These people and the types I have already described tend to look at the scientific answers which are our daily diet, that the Universe is so large that, from the billions of stars in it, we must have other Earths, with intelligent life resulting from the Big Bang. They believe that the probability is of death being final, and that being so it's probably best to spend the time we have on Earth selfishly indulging, as the possibility of afterlife is negligible.

I can categorically tell you that based on what I have told you and on much more that I have learned, I know now that my interpretation is correct and these people are so wrong.

This Earth is the only one that supports human life. It

was placed here for the purpose of selection; the many mansions exist for the selected sections of ourselves and those gone before.

Now then, Michael this is about as much as I am at the moment prepared to explain to you, I have I think given you most of my reasons for coming to these conclusions. I will let you get back to Ireland now safe in the knowledge that what I have divulged to you will help you with your mother, her being such a kind and generous soul.

There is much more to tell, however, on my eternal journey, but now you have listened to my story so far, I do hope that on our next meeting you will allow me to continue on the subject of the other side, explaining the various paths, that we face with their very different destinations along with other issues, clarifying reincarnation, spiritual time and many other fascinating scenarios. But these are for another day.

Now then, Michael, they are calling foot passengers on board, so I will leave you with one final thought before I leave you.

We entered this world with no history, but while we are here and after we leave, we have a responsibility to those left behind.

8 THE BEGINNING

The feeling of satisfaction that I now felt was immeasurable now that I was finally able to relax in the knowledge that I had, against all the odds, managed to put down on paper an account of my lifetimes strange experiences, taking into consideration that I am by no means an accomplished writer. I felt a sense of pride that all the experiences to which I refer had been documented only after the most careful thought and recall, because as I saw things, the story gave warnings to us all of our unavoidable futures.

Having said all this, I had found the difficulties of writing the account very stressful, and now looked forward to a well-earned rest. I must admit that I was secretly looking forward to a time when I would be able to carefully research the history of the old buildings of the tractor plant, along with the surrounding countryside and village, with the intention of possibly uncovering further relevant information.

I also hope that I would then be in a better position to document my conclusions as to what awaits us all on our departure from this life in accurate and fine detail.

Things change however, and true to form quicker than I would like. Let me explain what has just happened me, and what messages of warning it has brought.

I have now been put in a position, possibly by design, by a totally unexpected occurrence, sobering and frightening, with a veiled warning that I should document my conclusions immediately. I feel compelled to put pen to paper to conclude this final chapter as a sort of revelation of my story, I must add however, that I now feel as result of this latest information, suddenly immersed or bathed in light and understanding.

This all sounds strange, but let me explain. It had been several months since Michael had returned to Ireland, and thank God all now seems well with his mother and family. Hopefully the guidance I was able to give Michael had helped with the way he had handled things on his return.

Over here in England, we also got back to the normalities of life and settled down to the usual work rest and play of a normal family life.

Then it happened, several nights ago, nothing out of the ordinary had occurred for ages, life was back to normal and after supper, being a school day the family retired to bed at around 10:30 pm. I was the last to wearily climb into bed, switched on the small television set by the bedside, and fairly soon dropped off to sleep listening to the late news programme.

At exactly 2:00 am I was woken up, by what? I am not sure! But I was wide awake. This was very unusual for me, as I am, by nature, a good sleeper. I reached out and turned off the television, which was droning on with yet another news update, I glanced at my wife, but she was sound asleep.

I lay back down on the pillow and began to drift off to sleep again, but was brought fully round once more. This time by a steady flow of uncontrolled information, which is pouring into my brain. I felt that I have no control over what I was thinking, it was as if someone was speaking to me, but there was no audible voice, only the continual stream of information.

I suddenly started to begin to understand things, things which I had pondered upon all my life. Jigsaws were beginning to piece themselves together, the picture was clearing, the sheer intensity of this information seemed endless and its content amazing.

I soon realised that what was happening to me may

never happen again, and that what I was seeing must be documented. I was worried that if I fell asleep I would not be able to remember everything in detail the following morning, and so would lose the content of the messages I was receiving.

"Being Given". This was the key to the state I found myself in. You see I felt that I had no control over what I was visualizing, and that from wherever this information was coming from, I was meant to remember it all. I therefore decided to get out of bed and go downstairs to document what was coming through before anything could be forgotten.

I crept quietly downstairs, a strange feeling of not being alone accompanying me, but I pressed on finding the first notepad and pen to come to hand which was my wife's shopping notepad, luckily it was a newish one with plenty of unused pages as I had much to document.

I sat quietly on the settee busily noting down, not only the messages that I had so far received upstairs, but also other information which seemed to be coming to me since entering the lounge. I filled several pages of notes in what seemed to be a very short period of time. The messages stopped and rather than trying to make sense of it all I decided to return to bed, leaving the notebook on the arm of our settee.

On arriving back into our bedroom, it seemed to be only a matter of a few minutes before I was again in a deep sleep, hardly being able to keep my eyes open on the return journey upstairs.

It was not long however when I was awakened yet again with exactly the same stream of information pouring into my mind. I lay awake for several minutes soaking up this incredible information, before sliding out of bed so as not to disturb my wife and heading downstairs to again record the revelations for fear of forgetting anything by morning.

But this time, as I started to descend the staircase I had a feeling of not being alone, I felt an unseen presence near to me, also there was a strong vaguely familiar smell on the staircase, a smell I had associated with my mother when she had been in her last days, maybe something connected with her medication or illness and a smell that I have noticed several times since her passing.

Nevertheless, I pressed onto the lounge before putting pen to paper I made myself a strong cup of coffee to steady the nerves. I then made myself comfortable on the settee writing again quite speedily on the same notepad that I had used on my last expedition. After being downstairs a good half hour, I was just writing the last five words of my account of recollections when the television suddenly switched itself on. I froze, hardly daring to believe what was happening. I spied the television remote set a couple of metres away on the television stand. In other words nowhere near where I could have accidentally switched on the television. I forced myself to write the last word of the five and began to rise from the settee. As I did so the television switched itself off. The strange smell that I associated with mother became very intense, and although I love my mother and have never been one to be afraid of family, things associated with the unknown, I felt myself becoming terribly disturbed and scared.

I gingerly stood up and put down the notepad and emptied the still half cup of coffee that was not drunk down the sink. I crept over to the staircase and made my way upstairs. It was only when I entered our bedroom that I again felt safe. The smell had gone, the air felt warm and it was not long before I was back in bed and asleep.

The morning came and slowly the night's events came back to me. I looked through the scrawled difficult to read notes that I had hurriedly jotted down and realised that I must now document information for you all as a warning.

Reading through my hurriedly written notes, which remember, had been scrawled down on notepaper in no particular order, or even in a prepared way, I must say that I will do my best to give you the content, but tidied up to some extent to try to make the message more understandable. I will, however, keep the original notes in a safe place for anyone who wishes to see them in the original form, but now I will translate what came through.

Having spoken to many people and listened to many different opinions, it seems to me that we all scurry around living our lives around our families and friends, not really bothering to spend much time thinking about the big questions, "what is this all about?" "Why are we here?" etc., but strangely most of us secretly think that by looking at scientific evidence, and taking into consideration that the universe, being so vast, that the chances of there being alien civilizations such as ours must be a nailed on certainty, and it is therefore only a matter of time before we as an intelligent race contact a similar civilization.

We seem to also assume that we humans live to a maximum of 100 years or thereabouts, die and then cease to exist. It is only various diverse religious teachings that give us hope of something further to come after our death, but I do believe that most people are secretly of the opinion that we just die without there been further life of any description.

On both the above points I must point out now that categorically those are complete misconceptions, and that there is a God and a chance for us all of eternal life, also there are no other alien worlds.

There is a huge reason for this earth existing. The easiest way to explain this is that in Christian teachings, for example, it is said that after we die everyone will be judged, all of us, on Judgement Day. According to what I have been told, this is not quite correct.

My message is that rather than being judged after our deaths, that this earth and our life on this earth is our judgement, in other words, when we reach our final breath, we, all of us, will have mapped our futures whilst being on earth, through our past deeds and how we lived our lives.

It is sad to say that only a few souls get through this judgement, even having had the teachings of the Bible and other religious teachings, many have not heeded the warnings of the Commandments or the Beatitudes, choosing the paths of killing and greed, along with much of which I have spoken of in my earlier warnings.

Just a note here reader that I am writing this account as near as possible to what the messages to me were that night and in a sequence as they came, that is to say these messages do not always appear to follow as a normal story would.

It continues, I can see much clearer now, creation did not occur in a short time, a long time ago, now it has been going on "forever past". It is all about us, the expanding universe and still with its original intents.

Who knows really what has been happening over the last, many years, after all we can only recall our time here on earth, everything before that, if there was anything has been wiped from our earthly memories.

I am attempting now to get to an important but terribly difficult point to illustrate, even with the enlightenment that I was given that amazing night. I still find it hard to find an easy way to put it, but let's try.

If you remember in my early chapters, I explained that I could remember back to before I was born and how the orbs that I was part of, and could see, were fundamental in this story. I must also point out now that the coming of Christ and his teachings of the New Testament is also at the forefront of my attempts to explain things.

You have to understand that there has been human life on this planet for thousands and thousands of years. Each human life has a soul, but as the body dies the spirit leaves the body and continues to exist. I believe that from what I have witnessed that the spirit can take the form of an orb, at least when it is not within a living body.

I am being given to understand that up until the coming of Christ, that souls either born or unborn suffered no consequence, and even with the passage of time had no hope of eternal life as I am now being shown.

Things changed dramatically after the coming of Christ, his crucifixion and resurrection, no longer were the old Testament teachings the order of the day, no the New Testament, with its hope of eternal life, was the way for all mankind.

Jesus said, "I am the light, he who believeth in me shall have everlasting life", he also went on to teach that those who followed his ways and examples would be rewarded in heaven, but those who did not and committed sins as portrayed in such as the Commandments could not hope to partake in the promised paradise.

With this information, along with all the earlier evidence that I wrote earlier, and with the stark messages I received on that enlightening night, I have come to the conclusion that anyone being born on earth since the resurrection of Christ, now has a genuine chance of eternal life, which will mean spreading civilisation through God's expanding universe for eternity, without the uncaring, selfish, dangerous, souls that did not live a life of charity and following God's teachings whilst having their only one chance in the lifetime of judgement, which they have unwittingly squandered.

Pre-life existence is never revisited, in other words, the following life is eternal.

Everlasting and eternal, I have to say. We take our final breath on this earth and our judgement is final, no way of altering things now, no second thoughts, and certainly no more chances.

But there for the few, the joy of moving to eternal life in God's expanding universe, "my father's house has many mansions" or, the alternative for those who did not live their lives by his teachings of love for others, they have condemned themselves to an eternity of massive distress and regret, and for what, a single life time spent persecuting others who did not share their views, killing, murder or simply amassing wealth while others in this world were starving. Many other reasons for this eternal woe can be found. It is not surprising therefore that it is only a few souls that find everlasting life, but in spite of the odds being on the side of failure, I believe that we as an intelligent race, will in time come to realise we can only gain Paradise by living this life, thinking of the good of others and following the teachings of the New Testament.

Can you imagine what it must be like to spend an eternity going nowhere, alone, with only the thoughts and memories of our time spent on this earth, remembering the actions and paths we chose that caused us not to move through to the promised paradise of eternal happiness.

I had a vision of a dark, grey, cold stone lined room. The room had no windows, only a shaft of light no bigger than a pencil was able to semi illuminate the place. There were four stone shelves in the room, two to left and two to the right. On the shelves were human bones, dry and dusty. There was no door in the room to either enter or leave. All there was in the room was complete and utter silence.

I knew that this place was waiting for the next lost soul that had not passed through the Gates of Judgement, a soul that if it had heeded the many warnings given, such as "the eye of the needle or the woman's last coin", could have avoided this destiny of eternal misery and joined the triumphant souls which were eagerly moving forward with like-minded kind compassionate souls to now newly populate our God's truly wondrous expanding universe.

I must say that something about all this reminds me of a time when I was around 12 years old. I can remember vividly attending a religious instructions class at school one day and hearing the teacher during one of his lessons utter a sentence that I found quite profound, and have remembered that sentence the whole of my life. The sentence he uttered was "after death, moments continued make the bliss of hell of eternity". How fitting this sentence is now so many years on in the context of my story. The bliss of moving through to an eternity of happiness, working with others to populate God's wondrous creation, or to be alone, fully conscious and aware of why there is no hope of sharing in that happiness, and the realisation that an eternity of regret is beginning to unfold.

I would like to add this point that I believe that vision I had of the tomb of bones, was an illustration only of what befalls the fallen souls. It was only my way of interpreting what could possibly be meant by eternal damnation, or my profound thinking of what could possibly await the fallen.

The visions and messages that I received that night, which to some extent, I believe my mother's spirit was involved with bringing to me, also spoke of many other things which to some extent answered questions that I had sometimes pondered upon. The first being on Incarnation and as to why it had as a subject come up in my life. My understanding is now that if a person is taken from this life before having the chance to live long enough to be judged on anything, or indeed be ill or incapacitated, also restricting the ability to live a normal life along with its decision making opportunities, then reincarnation is the only way this particular soul can find its destiny. So after its earthly life expires the soul is returned in a new body, more often than not to the same family as it was with before. There are other reasons for reincarnation, but as I see it, they are not relevant to the message I am portraying.

The second question that was in my mind and has probably been in many others was when we complete our time on earth, and assuming that we have lived a good life enabling us to move through to the promised eternal future, do we again meet up with our earthly relatives, fathers, mothers sons and daughters. I can reassure those who are interested in the answer to this question that the answer is in the affirmative, and that this is indeed a huge reward for the compassion and kindness shown in the lives they lived to reach the place they now find themselves.

The messages to me were indeed strange and unexpected, but oddly enough they were quite simple and straightforward, mirroring closely the tales and experiences that I have written about previously. All the answers are in the Bible or all around us for all to see. There are many clues about us in nature, one of which was illustrated to me on the night of the messages, I will explain.

It was according to my notes on the second visit downstairs that I was given a message related to the understanding that in earlier lives that we have had on this earth, having now been born into the present life, which is intended to be our judgement, that we have no recollection of any of our previous existences nor of being born on this planet. We then live this life and based on the judgement of how we lived our life, we move on to the next, hopefully the one of eternal happiness. Now, I was told that there is an example of this in nature, and I recall thinking at the time that we should take this as one of nature's examples of a sign from God.

It involved a butterfly and it's life-cycle, the caterpillar stage being our earlier existence, then the transition to the cocoon, representing our time spent on earth, the judgement years as I am led now to understand, and a time spent with no recollection of any earlier existence. Then after the cocoon stage we have the emergence of a beautiful butterfly, ready to move gloriously into a new existence. This butterfly stage signifies the triumphant souls from those of us which by following the path of righteousness and love was rewarded with everlasting life in God's paradise, which is the rest of eternity spent exploring and populating his forever expanding wondrous universe. What a reward, never has there been anything to compare with this, but how well deserved by those who earned it, they will, with other triumphant souls go on to populate far away "mansions" with a past judgement genetic kindness.

Now going back to my early recollections, I spoke of a time in my existence when I could recall actually being a floating green orb and meeting up with a similar, but red, coloured orb, which I now believe was my twin sister in a time before our actual birth in this world. Although I have just written that the cocoon stage has no recollection of an earlier existence. I must point out now that I believe I was meant to be able to recall this meeting of souls and subsequent birth into this world so that I would, as I am doing now, have the information to give some warning and guidance to those who will listen.

I did in an earlier chapter speak of multitudes of these orbs or souls awaiting birth for a chance of salvation, and I have also mentioned that I have from time to time during my life had occasion to see or glimpse them.

It all now seems too simple to be true, but I believe, just as I have been told in the past, that all the answers are there for us to see, we just have to look for them. They are in God's teachings in various religions, they can be found in nature and also in many handed down legends. Remember earlier I spoken of my great-grandfather and his prophesies. He was strongly of the opinion that many of life's fundamental questions could be answered by reading the Bible. I do not think anything is really being hidden from the human race, only of any pre-existence and the reason for that is to make sure that only the good and deserving souls make it through to the next life.

Reading my accounts of my life and the conclusions that we now contemplate, many people would start to ask questions such as - How can a universe begin from nothing? Or where did God come from? I can only say that I myself, or anyone else on this earth does not have the type of intelligence to even start to contemplate such questions, but we do have enough intelligence to see where we must go from here, and who knows, someday we may be given the ability to answer those types of questions. For the moment though, it is not a question for me, I believe the universe has being here in some form or another, forever and I believe it is everlasting but only for those of us who take the right path, world without end.

In conclusion now, I must return to the night that I am writing about, when I was visited by the soul of my mother. I believe that following death a person's soul can stay on earth for some time. I believe it visits relatives, maybe to say goodbye and usually is about on the body's funeral and internment. I also believe that a small number of these souls, such as my mother, attempt to maybe let us know that they are about, and I believe many of you reading this may have witnessed something to which I refer.

I must now conclude that all that I have written in this account is true and I believe I have been positioned to write it all down as an extra warning and guidance to all.

I did however, if you remember, say that I would have liked to have written about the final stage of my book at a later stage, perhaps after investigating the background of the tractor plant, but because of the messages that I believe come from mother, I was compelled to write it all now.

Now just before I completed my notes I had the experience of the television turning itself first on, then off, as I previously spoke of, but if you remember, I said that I was just coming to the last five words. It is those five words that I believe are the reason that I have been pushed to complete my writings earlier than I had planned. So now I will reveal those last five words, but I will write down exactly what I wrote in the last paragraph of my notes that night. Here goes! Original!

It's strange, another spirited message has started and pressed me into this final story, I think maybe I don't have time to wait for part one to be published and then write part two at length, as I planned, for two reasons, one, to save at least a few souls, as I say earlier that values have changed and perhaps, "I don't have long myself."

ABOUT THE AUTHOR

Alfred Jones was born in 1951 to a father of German and mother of Danish descent. Shortly after the war his parents settled in a quaint village near Huddersfield, where he now lives nearby with his wife and son.

Printed in Poland
by Amazon Fulfillment
Poland Sp. z o.o., Wrocław